The Effect of Interactivity in e-Learning Systems

The Effect of Interactivity in e-Learning Systems

By

Luis Palacios and Chris Evans

CAMBRIDGE
SCHOLARS
PUBLISHING

The Effect of Interactivity in e-Learning Systems,
by Luis Palacios and Chris Evans

This book first published 2013

Cambridge Scholars Publishing

12 Back Chapman Street, Newcastle upon Tyne, NE6 2XX, UK

British Library Cataloguing in Publication Data
A catalogue record for this book is available from the British Library

ISBN (10): 1-4438-5050-0, ISBN (13): 978-1-4438-5050-6

TABLE OF CONTENTS

LIST OF FIGURES

LIST OF TABLES

ABSTRACT

This book is based on research conducted to investigate whether interactivity yields a learning effect when used appropriately in e-Learning Systems, and whether this effect enhances learning. The importance of interactivity for success in learning has always been paramount; however, little scientific evidence can be found to support this importance (Sims, 2003; Leiner & Quiring, 2008). Thus, the book provides evidence of the impact of interactivity on e-Learning Systems considering three main agents: the learner, the teacher and the system (educational triangle). A key element often found to be related to learning and the three previously-mentioned agents is the concept of feedback. The use of interactivity as part of a feedback mechanism for enhancing learning is well documented in this book. Three empirical studies are presented that investigated interactivity within the educational triangle. These three studies were conducted based on the framework of positivism and action research paradigms. The first study, entitled "Interactive Pedagogical Feedback", aimed to gather evidence for how highly interactive pedagogically-designed formative feedback enhances students' memory and understanding. The two student groups to which the interactive conditions were added showed a significant difference in the post-test scores. A one-way ANOVA with a Turkey HSD post hoc test for all pair-wise comparisons reveals a significant difference between the transfer and no condition scenario. The second study, entitled "Interactive Audio Feedback", examined whether the speed enhancements of oral feedback improve the conditions for the production of the lecturer's feedback and the quality of the feedback delivered to the students. The use of the interactive condition reduces by 40 to 65 per cent the time it usually takes to prepare feedback for final assignments, and an unpaired Student's *t*-test shows significant differences in the use of the two conditions. The final study, "Interactive Texting Feedback", took a pedagogical approach to provide formative feedback to a student audience using mobile text messages. It aimed to determine whether Interactive Texting Feedback enhances the learning experience within the e-Learning environment. Inferential analysis demonstrated good correlations in the use and benefits obtained by the introduction of the interactive mechanism. The results indicated that interactivity is critical in promoting and enhancing effective learning. Learning theories led by the generative theory of learning (Wittrock, 1974) and the principles of multimedia learning (Mayer, 2001) provide scientific explanation for these findings.

ACKNOWLEDGEMENTS

I would like to take this opportunity to present my sincere thanks to all the people that have supported, encouraged, and contributed to this publication.

It is not possible to adequately express my gratitude and deep feeling for my father Angel Custodio Palacios and my sister Durnes Palacios who both unfortunately passed way while working on this research. All this work is dedicated to their memories.

Finally, my loving thanks go to all members of my family for their silent but strong support.

CHAPTER ONE

INTRODUCTION

1.1 Introduction

Human-technology interactions rule our lives with a clear purpose such as enhancing our lifestyles or supporting our present relationship with machines. Such interactions have been an important element in all human activities, from the earliest times to the present. Interactivity is tied to a long history of successful human events. Today, when interactivity is a core component of technology, this tendency has not diminished; on the contrary, it is growing at the same speed, or maybe even faster than technology. In education, for example, Technology-Enhanced Learning (TEL) uses interactivity to facilitate learning practices that have become ubiquitous (Chan et al., 2006). Learners can select their educational material and study at the place, time and pace that suits them as individuals, enabling them to be active learners. The importance of interactivity for success in teaching has been seen as fundamental for a long time (Webster & Hackley, 1997). This importance is emphasised to such an extent that it is claimed that students with higher levels of interaction will obtain more positive and higher levels of achievement (Fulford & Zhang, 1993). This book offers the reader a great opportunity to study and understand the important role that interactivity plays in the development of educational technology. It takes those interested in the future of education to the centre stage to show significant studies where an interactivity effect enhances learning and empowers the learner. Results corroborate the above-mentioned intrinsic relationship between levels of interactivity and levels of achievements.

Interactivity is changing the way we behave by increasing an individual's control over his or her own learning (Rogers, 2000). Since the introduction of the Internet, information is now in the hands of more individuals, with predictable consequences. One important consequence is the elimination of the intermediary in most business, service, and even academic transactions. In business, for example, there has been a transfer of power from the advertising agency building the brand to the individual consumer (Einstein & Pollack, 2000). In the past, an agency forged a brand and delivered it to the consumer. In an unprecedented shift in paradigm, the consumer actually creates the brand over time using a variety of media resources. This paradigm shift is not exclusive to business, but it is seen in many other areas where individuals have been empowered with tools and decision-making power that were inaccessible before. The research in this book identifies interactivity as one of the essential factors that promote this paradigm shift. Technology in the hands of the learner requires mechanisms to ensure and validate the transfer of information. Several examples and experiments (see Chapter Four

Interactive Pedagogical Feedback) illustrate the support for such an important change in paradigm.

Interactivity is everywhere these days. If you walk into a library or a museum, there will be an interactive map with guided instructions. The television set was transformed a long time ago into an interactive TV to enhance the entertainment experience (Jiang et al., 2011). Interactivity provides the viewer with real-time interaction with the TV content production team to guarantee the best possible entertainment experiences, and the ability to watch, participate, influence and control what they see. The literature review in the book explores this ubiquitous nature of interactivity and indicates the important role interactivity has played in the design of instructional material (Mayer, 2005). In addition, feedback as a fundamental concept in teaching and learning has been investigated and its importance as an instrument in the improvement of education well documented (Smits et al., 2008).

1.2 Research background

In education, interactivity has changed the teacher and student roles (Rogers, 2000). The teacher-student relationship used to occur in a one-way direction, where students adopted a passive role. Today, this relationship has been transformed to a bidirectional exchange where students have an active position. Educators, to adapt to these innovative events, have also changed from instructional delivery to instructional design, and this has given birth to information technologists responsible for applying information technology to the content (Anson, 1999). Instructional designers, tied to this impressive chain of events, have moved from the educational philosophical approach of behaviourism to cognitivism, and then on to constructivism, in a systematic progression toward individualised instruction (Cooper, 1993). A conceptual map of the relationship among these learning theories can be seen in MISSING. However, the book goes beyond this graphical representation to explain how these theories have evolved as a result of different phenomena that have been left unexplained. For example, cognitive theorists consider that behaviourism reduces complex human behaviour to simple cause-and-effect. In their quest to demonstrate that inside the mind complex processes have an active participation in learning, they not only presented the insufficiencies of behaviourism but developed a conceptual framework that explains their perspective (Köhler, 1927). Nowadays, the explosion of information in this digital era is represented in a section of the book that describes how "connectivism" portrays a new model that establishes a revolutionary concept of learning. Learning in this context is taken from the external cause-effect relationship, and/or the processes inside the mind, and placed outside as the act of recognizing patterns shaped by complex networks (Siemens, 2006).

This philosophical shift in paradigm through technology has found the appropriate environment (e-Learning) in which to demonstrate its potential and interactivity, and this is being used in an unprecedented way to enhance learning. Interactivity, as the ability to respond contingently to the learner's actions (Beauchamp and Kennewell, 2010), has been positioned as an important instrument for promoting leaning.

e-Learning, as the educational environment based on technology, is an innovative concept focused on the individual. Tavangarian et al. (2004) highlight this particular characteristic when they define e-learning as "all forms of electronic supported learning and teaching, which are procedural in character and aim to effect the construction of knowledge with reference *to individual* experience, practice and knowledge of the learner". However, e-learning is still in its infancy and its adoption, as with the implementation of any new technology, faces issues, such as the reduced usage of technology as an instruction delivery method and the ineffective use of technology to support learning (Kahiigi et al., 2007). In addition, a related constraint that is reducing support for the constructivist approach are the needs for customization of the content and learning material, and for an interactive relationship between the learner and the content that is being instructionally defined.

Many e-learning implementations fail because they just mirror common objects from the physical world, such as books, in a digital environment, without considering the environment and contextual characteristics.

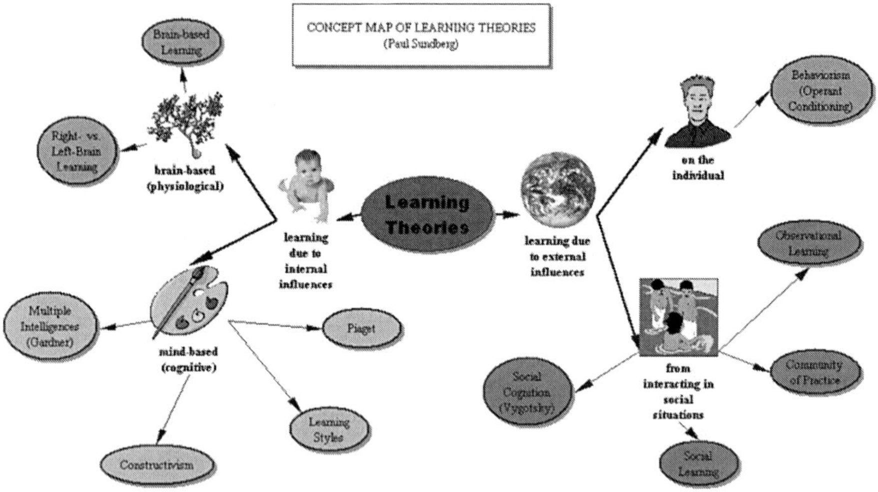

Figure 1: Concept Map of Learning Theories (Sundberg, P., 2003).

1.3 The research problem, aim and objectives

The challenge of this research is propelled by these emerging issues in e-learning that relate to interactivity. The main aim is to determine whether interactivity can enhance the learning experience by investigating its effects within a feedback context on three specific studies. The research undertakes this task by providing tangible evidence of the interactivity effects, identifying how interactivity affects the learning experience, and by investigating this effect within three different feedback contexts.

The importance of interactivity for success in learning has always been paramount. However, little scientific evidence can be found to support such a statement. Sims (2003), for example, comments that the concept of interactivity is frequently used to refer to an inherent quality of the medium and learning environment, with an underlying assumption that the interactive characteristics of communication with other learners or content objects is beneficial to the learning process. However, he does not perceive that tangible enlightenment is presented in the dynamics of interactivity. Leiner and Quiring (2008) argue that the user's perceptions of interactivity require more research as a central aspect in the new media context. The researchers previously mentioned clearly stated that the general perception is a lack of factual and scientific proof to support the argument. Thus, one of the research objectives is to provide this evidence.

This lack of evidence underpins the research and motivates the research question:

Can interactivity in an e-learning system enhance the learning experience?

Three main agents are identified in this process: the learner, the teacher and the system. Similar studies in the literature have called this relationship “the educational triangle” (Cumming, 1998; Wood et al, 1999). The effect of interactivity within these agents has been investigated to determine the impact on individualised learning.

An important element that also emerges from this question is related to interactivity and its ability to produce a learning effect when appropriately implemented in a particular system. Therefore, the research has the object of identifying how interactivity affects the learning experience in an e-learning setting. Since the main aim is the identification of learning as a result of the introduction of interactivity, the study of learning as a process of transferring knowledge is vital. Other effects may be present that enhance the learning experience given the reaction speed resulting from incorporating interactivity in another scenario or contextual situation.

Furthermore, this study has the object of investigating the effect of interactivity within a feedback context. Bransford et al. (2000) indicate that frequent feedback is essential for deep learning. Interactive feedback offers feedback quickly and at the appropriate frequency, to help keep motivation and interest in the topic taught. Feedback increases the amount of time dedicated to learning because it engages the learner in an interactive learning process. Research indicates that the time dedicated to learning is essential because it is approximately proportional to the amount of material being learned (Singley and Anderson, 1989).

Feedback is information communicated to improve learning by changing thinking or learner behaviour (Shute, 2008). The use of interactivity as part of a feedback mechanism for enhancing learning is well documented in the literature. Feedback is essential for learning because it is information communicated to improve learning by changing the learner’s thinking or behaviour. Three empirical studies were designed to investigate the effect of interactivity within the previously mentioned educational triangle.

The first empirical study revolves around the concept of using formative feedback pedagogically designed to enhance learner skills. It is believed that interactivity incorporated into a computer-based system in the form of formative feedback will increase learning. Knowledge about appropriately implementing and embedding formative feedback within learning environments has recently taken more relevant position recently

(Bell & Cowie, 2001). Information about feedback and its characteristics is also highly important; for example, immediate constructive feedback offers a valuable contribution to the learning experience, but if feedback is provided too soon it seems to block relevant mental information processing activities and thus degrades learning (Requin & Stelmach, 1991).

The second study relates to enhancing teachers' capabilities to produce effective and quicker interactive feedback using audio, as for most people speaking is a much quicker form of communication than typing. These speed enhancements of speaking rather than typing are carried over to the process of creating feedback to enhance learning-related activities. The expansion of higher education has meant that, with large numbers of students, producing feedback can be a very time consuming task. This can have a knock on effect on the length and quality of individual feedback. There is a need, therefore, to find mechanisms to ensure that the quality and quantity of feedback is sustained or even enhanced.

The final study focuses on the system. It mediates the relation between the two main agents of the educational triangle: the teacher and the learner. The empirical study uses text messages (SMS) supported by a web-based response system to provide formative feedback to a student audience after educational content has been delivered. The objective of this experiment was to determine whether Interactive Texting Feedback is a valid and effective pedagogical approach to enhance the learning experience. The feedback system employed to communicate with teachers and learners is a logical and direct way to integrate technology with pedagogical practices and learning activities. Interactivity, as the essential component in technology, plays a key role in communication among the agents of this educational triangle.

1.4 The contribution of this research

From a theoretical point of view the book contributes to a conceptual framework for the understanding of interactivity in e-learning systems, identifies the important role interactivity has taken in all learning activities mediated by technology, and illustrates the implications of using interactivity within the educational triangle: the teacher, the learner and the system. The information contained in the book is useful for academics and institutions to improve their teaching, guide the design of instructional content and the efficiency of their learning delivery mechanisms. It could also be of utility to other researchers, or those in roles that require an understanding of interactivity.

Previous studies attribute apparent success or lack of success to enhance learning by using interactivity. This research also contributes from a practical perspective with significant evidence of the tangible effect of interactivity within the three particular agents of the educational triangle that combine in any learning experience. Moreover, the book constitutes a road map for those practitioners, lecturers, etc., interested in the design and implementation of sound academic content, production of audio feedback, and blending learning.

The contribution of the work described in this book has been recognised through the peer-reviewed publication of sub-sections of it in the following journals and conferences: Cases on Transnational Learning and Technologically Enabled Environments (book published by IGI Global (Palacios & Evans, 2010)); Conference on Innovations in Learning for the Future 2010: e-Learning in Istanbul, Turkey, (Palacios & Evans, 2010); International Journal of E-Adoption (Evans & Palacios, 2011); Fifth Mediterranean Conference on Information Systems MCIS 2010 (Evans & Palacios, 2011); 2010 International Conference in Cairo, Egypt. (Evans & Palacios, 2011); The International Conference in Education and Management Technology (ICEMT) (Evans & Palacios, 2011) and in the International Conference IADIS e-Learning 2011, Rome, Italy (Evans & Palacios, 2011).

1.5 The overall structure of the book

The overall structure of the book is designed around the concept of interactivity and how it enhances learning in three different feedback scenarios. This chapter has described the scope of this book by presenting the research background about interactivity, identified the research problem, the significance of this research, and the methodology to be followed to answer the research questions and to test the proposed hypotheses, and explain the overall structure of the book.

Chapter 2 reviews the literature in the areas of e-learning, interactivity, feedback delivery and the theoretical background to support the research. Major philosophical approaches are explained in this literature review to support these different perspectives of how people learn and how teachers educate. These teaching strategies vary across disciplines and they are conceived as pedagogical information that help students overcome difficulties and guide them through a typical path in order to achieve understanding.

Chapter 3 describes in general the methodology followed to provide validity and reliability to the research.

The next three chapters describe the experiments designed to test the effects of interactivity within feedback mechanisms embedded in the context of the educational triangle. Chapter 4 is about interactive pedagogical feedback. It focuses on the learner and how interactivity enhances his/her cognitive abilities. This empirical study is conducted to test the first hypothesis that interactivity in the form of retention and transfer ISAQ incorporated in a computer-based system increases learning.

Chapter 5 is about Interactive Audio Feedback for Enhancing Learning. Teachers' capability to produce quality feedback is enhanced by producing it in half the time that it takes to produce normal feedback. The Interactive Audio feedback study was designed to test the two following hypotheses: that "creating feedback in audio form is quicker than creating feedback in typewritten form" and "that feedback received in audio form is better quality than feedback received in written form".

Chapter 6 is more related to the mediator system in the pedagogical triangle. The Interactive Texting Feedback study uses action research methodologies to determine the effectiveness of interactivity in this context. It responds to the final hypothesis that interactive texting feedback is an effective approach to enhance learning practice.

And finally, Chapter 7 embraces a general discussion of the results found in the three experiments designed to test the effects of interactivity. It generalises the findings and relates to the appropriate theories to explain the phenomenon. It then addresses the limitations of this study and suggests directions for future research. Lastly, the conclusion is presented.

CHAPTER TWO

THE EFFECT OF INTERACTIVITY IN e-LEARNING SYSTEMS

2.1 Introduction

The present section considers the relevant literature relating to the effects of interactivity in different e-learning systems or TEL mechanisms. TEL refers to the support of any learning activity through technology (Manouselis et al., 2011) and is usually used synonymously with the term e-learning, although they do differ as TEL focuses largely on the technological support of any pedagogical approach that utilises technology. Although the utilisation of TEL is new, research on the subject has spanned three generations (Hakkarainen, 2009): the first generation studied computer-assisted learning from a cognitive perspective; the second-generation research focused on analysing patterns of participation (social view) in computer-assisted learning; and the third generation of research aimed to overcome the disparity between the cognitive (knowledge acquisition) and socio-cultural (participation) perspectives. This chapter establishes the bases for understanding the theoretical background supporting the research in interactivity and its effects in learning presented in this book. An explanation of e-learning is therefore relevant as the main environment where the research is going to take place.

e-Learning is a term that encompasses all forms of TEL, but tends to focus on pedagogy (Watkins, 2010). Indeed, e-learning is predicted to be the mechanism by which future students and organisations can facilitate learning practices that are independent of time, place and pace (Palacios & Evans, 2010a; Zhang et al., 2004). For example, educational technologies empower individuals in gaining international access to the academic resources of countries in which self-directed study and student autonomy are emphasised (Ziguras, 2001). Learners can select educational material and study in accordance with their own style and pace, enabling them to be active learners. The flexibility provided by these interactive technologies does not constrain the learner in terms of location or time. Furthermore, it facilitates a more active role and personal development, and generally involves the support of any learning activity by means of technology. These learning activities are organised with the intention of improving students' knowledge, skills and competence.

According to Stergioulas (2004), there is a need to improve and consolidate the professional learning of the current learning systems that are seen in research policies and road maps designed for e-learning Technologies in Europe. In this context, e-learning is seen as a tool that minimises the time needed to prepare for future jobs in order to improve the current knowledge base and expertise and transform the process of continuous professional development.

Interactivity is a distinctive component within the modern world of technology, and, as an educational tool, it is perhaps the element that offers the best guarantee in education (Domagk, Schwartz & Plass, 2010). People have been interacting with their environment, absorbing knowledge or creating new experiences on top of previous ones from an early age (Hofer & Pintrich, 1997). Learning is considered the transformational process of increasing abilities to obtain goals (Washburne, 1936), and thus people and technology interaction are relevant within the process of learning. The extension and effect of these interactions has in learning are not well known. In addition, the effect of interactivity is vaguely registered in the literature from an academic perspective. Thus, the research developed in the chapters following intend to provide evidence of the types of effect interactivity cause in learning. Practical activities in real academic scenarios but under scientific control are evaluated and presented in next chapters.

Since the focus on learning alternatively shifts from technology to human cognition in order to take into account our ability to assimilate knowledge (Zuga, 2004), it is sensible to study several theories and concepts of learning in order to gain a better understanding of these issues and to support this research. Moreover, there is a paradigm shift (Rogers, 2000) from "teaching" to "learning" promoted by technology that has been evolving in recent decades. Fantuzzo (1992), for example, described the use of behavioural analysis in education to indicate that a teacher-centred approach was the cornerstone of resolving the educational challenges of that generation. In contrast, Geelan (2001) advocated the notion of "student-centred learning" as a popular and influential approach for students to control and develop own educational activities in a more constructivist framework. Interactivity seems to be at the centre of this paradigm shifting.

A great variety of learning theories have enriched the realm of education and other disciplines, but they overlap and coincide in their final outcome of learning (Guild, 1997). Learning theories moved into the psychological and sociological processes a long time ago, in the search for general ways to explain how we learn and how to do it more effectively (Zito & Schout, 2009). A learning theory is a method that describes how people learn and the complexity of the process of learning (Leonard, 2002).

There are four main philosophical approaches presented in this section that encompass a huge body of learning theories. Behaviourism, cognitivism and constructivism (see Figure 1) **follow a natural path of evolution from an emphasis on the environment** (behaviourism) **to an emphasis on the internal complexities of human learning** (cognitivism and constructivism) (Cooper, 1993). Nevertheless, an emergent approach named "connectivism" has come to emphasise how influential the use of network technology can be in learning (Siemens, 2005).

Behaviourism largely focuses on the observable changes of learner behaviour, while cognitive theories go beyond behaviour and explain mind-based learning. Constructivism considers learning as a phenomenon in which the learner actively constructs or builds new ideas or concepts. Connectivism on the other hand argues that learning today is too complex to be processed in the above-mentioned way. There is therefore a need to rely on the learning externally embedded within a network of people and/or technology that store, access, and retrieve knowledge (Siemens, 2006).

Furthermore, the experiments presented in the book were designed taking into account the principles that underpin these theories. For example Chapter Four Interactive Pedagogical Feedback investigates the concept presented in the cognitive model of learning (Sweller, 1988) to envisage a new mechanism to enhance memory's capacity. However, there is no intention to apply in this research the entire theoretical concepts presented in this literature review. They intend to illustrate how they have evolved and how they are interconnected with each other. The following sections in this chapter will present a more complete explanation of each of these theories.

2.2 Learning as Behaviour

Behaviourists concentrate on observing changes in behaviour (Skinner, 1953). Indeed, behaviourism is a theory of learning that mainly focuses on the observable changes in learner behaviour and discounts mental activities. Behaviour theorists consider learning as nothing more than the acquisition of new behaviour, and Skinner (1953) was influential in defining behaviourism. The theory identifies conditioning as the main element of the learning process and, according to Skinner (1953), classic conditioning and behavioural or operant conditioning are the two different types of conditioning.

Classic conditioning occurs when a physiological reaction is triggered by a stimulus (Figure 2). Pavlov (1906) highlights how one can change the stimulus part of a stimulus-response pattern (such as salivation) to something neutral (such as turning on a light), and yet generate the same response. Pavlov observed that the dogs started to salivate as soon as they saw the person who usually brought the food, enabling him to demonstrate that any neutral stimulus could be associated with food and thus elicit the food response, even when no food was present. The original stimulus and response to this stimulus are the "unconditioned stimulus" and the "unconditioned response", with the introduced neutral stimulus and learned response known as the "conditioned stimulus" and the "conditioned response", respectively. Pavlov's work on the accumulation of information and classical conditioning has been continued, but Bitterman (2006) considers there has been little conceptual progress. From the classical conditioning perspective (Pavlov, 1906), learning activities and the context in which they are performed should create or promote pleasant emotions, such as enthusiasm, excitement or enjoyment. These emotions will motivate learners in the completion or better performance of any learning task and will ensure that they actively participate in the experience. Another educational implication of behaviourism relates to measuring the impact of changes on behaviour. Evaluation thus plays a fundamental role in determining that learning has taken place. Behavioural or Operant Conditioning occurs when a response to a stimulus is reinforced and operant conditioning can be considered a feedback system: if the presence of a reward or reinforcement follows the response to a stimulus, then the response becomes more probable in the future. Skinner (1953; Skinner, 2009) used reinforcement techniques to teach pigeons to dance and bowl a ball in a mini bowling-alley. Behaviourism has been used for a significant period of time to encourage positive behaviour and deter negative behaviour (Ormrod, 2004).

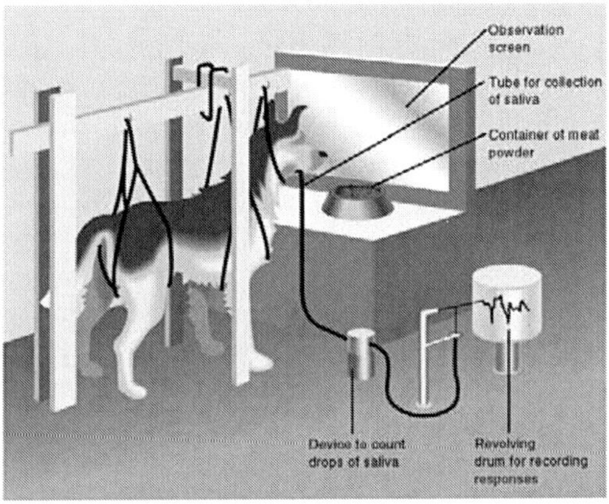

Figure 2: Classic Conditioning

In terms of *operant conditioning*, cultivating good habits through the repetition of stimulus-response exercises is part of normal classroom activities: the use of reinforcement and punishment constitutes a fundamental component in contemporary education, and is derived from the practice of behaviourism. Rewards that reinforce positive behaviour in order to increase the probability of a response, such as publicly praising students' skills and the recommendation of special projects, are the hallmarks of a good teacher. Positive reinforcement involves the presentation of the stimulus after the response, while negative reinforcement is employed to prevent or avoid an adverse condition; for example, submitting all assignments on time results in the lowest grade being avoided. This increases a response through the removal of the stimulus, which is usually an adverse or unpleasant one: for example, the removal of anxiety can be a very important negative reinforcer. Although positive and negative reinforcement increases learner responses, punishment decreases the responses expected; this is because punishment involves presenting a strong stimulus that decreases the frequency of a particular response. Thus, punishment is quite useful in quickly eliminating undesirable behaviours; an example of this is late assignments being given a zero grade.

Interactivity is connected to the behaviourist concept and Skinner's (1953) idea that information should be presented in small amounts has had a profound impact on educational software in which reinforcement plays a fundamental role: increasing the frequency of reinforcement by reducing the size of the information presented yields more effective results (Sims,

1996). In fact, early authoring tools for programmed instruction modules were originally designed in line with behaviourist principles. Corrective feedback, consistently used by behaviourists, is also a fundamental component of multimedia design. According to Hartsell (2006), interactivity is implemented in tutorials, using corrective feedback, in order to reward learners who accurately answer questions with audible comments. Gagne's (1962) work with the military strongly influenced the design of instructional materials and the development of instructional software. Through his work, Gagne stated how the interaction only allowed students to respond to questions posed by the instructor.

However, the application of behaviourism principles fails to address two important concerns in instructional design (Chase, 1985). The first is the lack of effective implementation of technology tools, such as computers and interactive media. To overcome this, realistic educational implementations had to be developed. The other is the production of low-level skills programmes that are unable to represent complex conceptual behaviour. These factors were borne in mind while designing and developing the experiments implemented in the book because they were considered relevant in keeping the research up to date. Since behaviourist ideas are outdated, the inclinations on the research fell into more technological orientated approaches.

2.3 Cognitive Theory

Cognitive learning theory describes how people or animals learn by understanding their mental processes and how they organise, store and relate old and new information, scripts and schema (Sweller & Chandler, 1994). Cognitive theory refuses to accept behaviourism as the only explanation for the human acquisition of knowledge, believing that behaviourism reduces complex human behaviour to simple cause-and-effect. In their quest to present the insufficiencies of behaviourism, gestalt psychologists (Köhler, 1927) demonstrate the pitfalls of the behaviourist concept of learning in their experiments to show that people are simply not programmed entities that respond to environmental stimuli: they are rational beings that require active participation in order to learn and their actions are a consequence of the processes developed in their minds. Behaviour is a manifestation of what takes place in the learner's mind. The shift from behaviourism to cognitivism occurs gradually, and Hartley (1985) based it on the short- and long-term memory paradigm.

In order to understand a wide range of cognitive functions, the constructs of working memory (WM), short-term memory (STM) and long-term (LTM) memory are central to the cognitive learning theory. However, there is a lack of consensus in the literature in what these constructs represent, and how to distinguish them from one another. Terms such as "memory" and "storage capacity" are part of the cognitive vocabulary and are part of the computer jargon terminology. In the computer industry, memory is a part of a computer in which information is stored for immediate use by the central processing unit. Storage capacity is related to the maximum number of bits, bytes, words, or items that can be held in a memory system (Collins, 2000). "Memory" and "storage capacity" usage is similar in a cognitive context. People's memory is determined by the limit in the duration for which an item can remain active in STM without rehearsal (Cowan, 2001). Although memory capacity to storage is seven chunks (Miller, 1956), depending on people's differences this can increase or decrease by two chunks. Chunking, in psychology, is a phenomenon whereby individuals group responses when performing a memory task.

In addition, storage capacity is time-limited rather than capacity limited (Cowan, 2001). Rose et al. (2010) attempted to differentiate these constructs by comparing the effects of depth of processing on WM and LTM using a levels-of-processing (LOP) span task procedure that involved processing to-be-remembered words based on their visual, phonological or semantic characteristics. Rose et al. concluded that WM involved retrieval from LTM memory, and that it is affected by the match (or mismatch) between initial processing and subsequent retrieval.

The term working memory implies a system for the temporary holding and manipulation of information during the performance of a range of cognitive tasks, such as comprehension, learning and reasoning (Baddeley, 1986). Indeed, the term is used interchangeably to describe what is also called STM, primary memory, immediate memory, operant memory or provisional memory. WM emphasises the notion of the manipulation of information rather than passive maintenance (Atkinson & Shiffrin, 1968) and can be considered a more dynamic and complex STM construct (Baddeley & Hitch, 1974). Recently, Baddeley suggested that WM may be considered as an interface between STM and LTM, and thus he modified his original model by adding a new component, the episodic buffer, in order to accommodate the way in which WM and LTM interact.

It is important to emphasise that the interaction between storage and processing is controlled by selective attention to the subset of elements in working memory that may be manipulated at any moment. The mind's ability to direct its inner awareness upon a particular target in WM has been the predominant focus of attention (Cowan, 1995). Cowan (1995) and other researchers (Baddeley, 1986) believe that WM is activated information along with central executive processes. They have therefore developed a framework that integrates attention and memory. The focus of attention capacity has a limit of about one element (Garavan, 1998); however, it can be expanded to four elements with practice (Oberauer, 2006). Interactivity plays a fundamental role in this practice, as demonstrated in the experiment developed by Verhaeghem (2005). Within this framework, WM consists of three embedded components: the activated part of long-term memory, the region of direct access and the focus of attention.

Working memory is used as an area for the storage of short-term information, including separate auditory and visual working memories (Baddeley, 1986). In later research, Baddeley (1992) asserted that the working memory is organised into a visual-spatial sketch pad for visual image manipulation and the phonological loop, which handles speech-based information.

Short-term memory, however, is used to retain information for short periods. WM and STM are considered different constructs, but are highly related (Engle et al., 1999). In fact, the two constructs have been used synonymously for so long that many of the tasks depicted in the literature as working memory tasks reflect a common construct. The short-term store has a working memory component, a sort of mental notepad that is used to manipulate information in consciousness. STM refers to the activated elements in this memory model, whereas WM is a larger component that incorporates the activated elements and the executive processes.

STM is related to the current contents of consciousness, while LTM comprises memories previously encoded in the remote past that must be brought back into consciousness through the retrieval process (Atkinson & Shiffrin, 1968). LTM has no known limit to its storage capacity, and verbal elements are normally coded in terms of their semantic characteristics (Craik & Lockhart, 1972). Thus, information stored in the LTM is very sensitive to the depth to which memory items are processed when they are initially encoded. Structural memory items, such as phonological or visual elements, usually lead to lower levels of retention than semantically processed memory items such as concepts (Craik & Lockhart, 1972). Long-term memory is the resident knowledge and skills acquired and held in a permanently retrievable area.

In summary, a cognitive model of learning (Sweller, 1988) is built based on three memory types: sensory memory, working memory, and long-term. These memories have limited capacity. Sensory and working memory holds much less information than long-term memory, which is considered a huge reservoir for data accumulation. Interactivity seems to play an important role in connecting knowledge stored in LTM with information in sensory and working memory. The research in this book considers how this connection occurs and introduces interactivity within the design of educational material to measure its effects in Chapter FourInteractive Pedagogical Feedback.

Cognitive learning theory focuses on the internal processes of the human brain. Mental processes, such as thinking, memory, knowing and problem solving, are portrayed as schemata that are considered symbolic mental constructions (Anderson, 1982). A schema is an active organization of past reaction or past experiences (Anderson & Pearson, 2002) that can be modified to accommodate new mental information. Thus, learning is a change in the learner's schemata. These intellectual processes, categorised as "information processes", bear a resemblance to computer operations and thus the terminology used is the same whether applied to psychology or computer science. The learner, in this theory, is considered an information processor and is analogous to a computer.

As learning theories have proliferated to encompass different ways of learning in recognition of the fact that no one learns in the same way, cognitive theory has diversified to explore our inner mind and tackle other specific situations. Thus, the cognitive load theory (Chandler & Sweller, 1992), the dual-coding theory, the generative learning theory and the theory of multimedia learning are approaches that must be mentioned, as they are related to this work.

Feinburg and Murphy (2000) defined cognitive load theory as "the amount of mental energy" required for processing a given amount of information. As the amount of information increases, so does the cognitive load on our mental resources. If the amount of information and instruction surpasses the capacity and limitations of our mental resources, learning does not take place and our sensors become distorted.

Paivio's (1986) dual-coding theory establishes that verbal and non-verbal information is represented in different mental systems. These systems use working memory to process the received information, as words and pictures activate independent visual and verbal codes. When information is highly imaginable, a learner can encode the information into long-term memory (LTM), using both a verbal and visual trace. This redundant encoding increases the probability of future retrieval, because if one memory trace is lost (whether visual or verbal), the other is still available (Rieber, 1990).

One important concept also related to constructivist views of learning explaining the investigation in this research is the generative learning theory. Wittrock (2010; 1974) indicates in this theory that learning is the result of concrete associations which the learner generates between his prior experience (stored in LTM) and the stimuli. It's the process of constructing relationships between new and old knowledge that supports the individual's understanding of how new ideas fit into his mental web of known concepts. He emphasized that the learner is not a passive recipient of information but an active participant in the learning process working to construct meaningful understanding of information found in the environment. Interactivity in this context seems to take a relevant role in the generation of the schemata mentioned previously that explains how new conceptual understanding is formed. The discussion in section in 4.4 of the book associates the theory with the empirical results obtained.

2.4 Constructivist Learning Theory

Constructivism is the tag given to a group of theories that argue that humans generate knowledge and meaning from the interaction between their experiences and their ideas. The core theory of constructivism was established by Vygotsky (1978), who emphasised that social interaction is the principal factor in the cognitive progress. Vygotsky's work has been the foundation of developmental cognition and constructivist theories for the past 50 years. Constructivism proposes that the learner is much more actively involved in interacting with the teacher in generating new meanings. Constructive learning takes place when meaningful mental representations are constructed on top of previous knowledge-creating schemata; therefore, learning is the active, contextualised process of constructing rather than a passive acquisition of knowledge, and instruction is the process of supporting the knowledge constructed by the learners rather than the mere communication of knowledge (Duffy & Cunningham, 1996; Honebein, Duffy, & Fishman, 1993; Jonassen, 1999).

The two views of the theory distinguish between cognitive constructivism and social constructivism (Vygotsky, 1978). The former focuses on how learners acquire knowledge as a result of developmental psychology and learning styles, and considers that knowledge incites further cognitive development, while the latter attempts to explain learning acquisition and how understanding is generated through social interaction. Social interaction and social context are essential in cognitive development, particularly when progressing from childhood. A child's cultural development is first established on a social level, as a result of interaction with people (inter-psychological) and later on an individual level, within the child (intra-psychological). All the higher functions originate as actual relationships between individuals. For example, Vygotsky (1978) found that children interacting with older individuals were able to perform better.

There are two important aspects in understanding how Vygotsky's (1978) work is relevant to this research, as they define how people's interactions underpin their learning acquisition. These are the More Knowledgeable Other (MKO) and the Zone of Proximal Development (ZPD). These concepts are used in the experiments as part of the theoretical background to support the research.

The MKO refers to someone (a peer) or something (a computer system) that has a better understanding or a higher level of ability than the learner, in terms of a particular activity, procedure or concept. Concerning Vygotsky's original view, the notion of the MKO refers to school children. Thus, one can infer that the MKO is a teacher or an older adult; however, a child's peers could constitute individuals with more knowledge or experience. However, the term is often used in the literature in different contexts, such as peers as learners (Van Lier, 2000) and does not have to refer to a person. Indeed, it may allude to a learning content management system that supports employees in their learning process: computer-assisted tutors have been used in educational settings, in order to facilitate and guide students through the learning process.

The Zone of Proximal Development (ZPD) is the difference between what a learner can do individually and what the same learner can do with the help of the MKO. Vygotsky's (1978) research determined that intelligence can be measured by comparing individual learning skills in solving or understanding a problem with the same learner skills used to solve problems with the assistance of someone who has mastered the concepts previously. The idea of using unique means to measure learner intelligence goes against the concept of ZPD, which rejects the application of standardised tests (Berk & Winsler, 1995a; Berk & Winsler, 1995b).

Vygotsky's (1978) research focuses on how children's functions (such as attention, memory and perception) develop and are individual to the learner. Children can do and understand more with the help of adults who provide apprenticeships in acquiring skills than they can do on their own. This is apparent in the classroom, where the teacher, as the most knowledgeable member of the class, has a fundamental role in employing a variety of tools and scaffolds to support the development of academic activities, e.g. reading and writing (Gallimore, Goldenberg & Weisner, 1993). Therefore, the range of skills that children may develop usually surpasses what they could attain on their own. Further investigation has revealed that the quality of learning through mediation is attributed to human beings. It can be said that, in a variety of ways, adults mediate the world for children and teach them how to get the most from it.

Within the Vygotskian (Vygotsky, 1978) concept of the zone of proximal development, social interaction is the basis for cognitive growth. As with many significant theories in the academic world, the concept of ZPD has been expanded and turned into new ideas since Vygotsky's original research and extended into concepts like scaffolding and the Zone of Reflective Capacity (ZRC).

Scaffolding refers to the process whereby an MKO supports and helps students in their ZPD as necessary, diminishing this aid as and when it becomes unnecessary. The ZRC (Tinsley & Lebak, 2009) is related to the ZPD, but targets it in more detail and guides the way in which an adult's capacity for reflection can expand when collaborating with other adults with similar goals over an extended period of time.

The previous concepts underpin constructivist learning, which occurs when learners actively build meaningful mental representations from the presented information (Mayer et al., 1999). Active construction processes involve selecting relevant phrases and image sequences; in terms of the presented material, organising them into coherent causal chains (known as internal connections) and relating them to mental prior knowledge (Mayer & Moreno, 1998a; Mayer et al., 1999). In this context, hypermedia, simulation, virtual reality and open-ended learning environments are beneficial in exploring and acquiring information more effectively.

In "Chapter Six Interactive Texting Feedback", for example, learning was influenced and constructed by the social context where it was taking place. Learners' text messages in this study were collected in a central website that reflected the opinion of the classroom. Thus, students could immediately compare their answer and validate it.

Constructivism, cognitivism and behaviourism portray learning as a process of changing performance or attitude due to the acquisition of skills or knowledge internally in the learner, but fail to address the fact that there are other learning processes that occur external to the learner, and resulting from the immense knowledge creation of the present digital society. Connectivism addresses this issue in the following section. Although a debate is taking place in this regard, it is considered in this research that Connectivism will be highly influential in the future of education.

2.5 Connectivism Learning Theory

According to Siemens (2004), connectivism considers learning as "actionable knowledge", and emphasises that learning occurs in the space between knowledge and meaning-making on the knowledge hierarchy. It is thus of vital importance for learning to make sense of the space in which the learner functions and the potential implications of acquired knowledge. This conceptualization of learning goes beyond the traditional view of learning as a mechanism for acquisition of knowledge. Driscoll (2000), for example, defined learning as "a persisting change in human performance or performance potential … as a direct result of the learner's experience and interaction with the world". It thus highlights the relevance of interactivity as a subject in this research. Connectivism is concerned with the huge amount of information available in the connected network and the speed this information is changing. A network in this regard is defined as connections between entities. In this context, it is very important for individuals to be able to filter content to determine valuable and on time information capable of altering the decision-making process.

Connectivism emphasises that knowledge resides not only in the mind of individuals, but also in a distributed manner across network nodes (Siemens, 2006). Learning in this context is the act of recognizing patterns shaped by complex networks. The networked act of learning exists on two levels: at an internal level, learning is represented as neural networks (where knowledge is distributed across our brain look Cognitive Theory); and at an external level, learning is depicted as networks we actively form (each node represents an element of specialization and the aggregate represent our ability to be aware of, learn, and adapt to the world around).

According to Wittgenstein (as cited in Siemens, 2006), the privacy of the internal mental processes or constructions attach an occult character or hidden power to the cognitive process of generating or assigning meaning. His investigations about the public and private nature of this process brought him to the conclusion that "systematic patterns of usage" are the primary expression of meaning.

Externalization of the process of generating meaning from the perspective that a "systematic pattern of usage" can be considered and recognised outside out mind add certain clarity to the process of meaning creation (Bloor, 1983).

Siemens has defined the following principles of Connectivism:

- Learning and knowledge rests in diversity of opinions;
- Learning is a process of connecting specialized nodes or information sources;

- Learning may reside in non-human appliances;
- Capacity to know more is more critical than what is currently known;
- Nurturing and maintaining connections is needed to facilitate continual learning;
- Ability to see connections between fields, ideas, and concepts is a core skill;
- Currency (accurate, up-to-date knowledge) is the intent of all connectivist learning activities.

Table 1 (below) represents the relationship between the traditional theories (see above) and connectivism.

Property	Behaviourism	Cognitivism	Constructivism	Connectivism
How does learning occur?	Black box—observable behaviour main focus	Structured, computational	Social, meaning created by each learner (personal)	Distributed within a network, social, technologically enhanced, recognizing and interpreting patterns
Influencing factors	Nature of reward, punishment, stimuli	Existing schema, previous experiences	Engagement, participation, social, cultural	Diversity of network
What is the role of memory?	Memory is the hardwiring of repeated experiences—where reward and punishment are most influential	Encoding, storage, retrieval	Prior knowledge remixed to current context	Adaptive patterns, representative of current state, existing in networks
How does transfer occur?	Stimulus, response	Duplicating knowledge constructs of "knower"	Socialization	Connecting to (adding) nodes
Types of learning best explained	Task-based learning	Reasoning, clear objectives, problem solving	Social, vague ("ill defined")	Complex learning, rapid changing core, diverse knowledge sources

Table 1: Learning Theories (Siemens, 2006).

Memory has a major role in the learning process, especially in cognitivism, which has been challenged by many technology tools more effective at retrieval than human beings. The book in fact demonstrates techniques to enhance our memory abilities, and is concerned in the three studies presented inside with the process of knowledge transfer and/or construction. Connectivism, on the other hand, is focused on the process of forming and creating meaningful networks including technology-mediated learning. It surpasses the argument of how knowledge is formed in our own minds to concentrate on linking to knowledge sources. Connectivism is the examination of ideas about how knowledge can be created by human minds either in corporations, computer devices, etc., may point to the future tendency of learning.

2.6 Interactivity

Interactivity is an important element in learning supported by technology (Lipponen, 2002). The term has evolved through time in a manner that is used in different contexts. Two of these dissimilar contexts are presented: one related to pedagogy and the other concerning new technologies in education (Beauchamp & Kennewell, 2010). In the former, interactivity and pedagogy have a long history together. Interaction between the teacher and the students is standard for an effective pedagogy (Doherty & Hilberg, 2007). Doherty (2007), for example, claims that the students' gain was greater in classrooms where teachers used effective pedagogies in the classroom than in other classrooms without it. In the latter, student-teacher interaction has evolved to be considered an essential component of any e-learning system (Palacios & Evans, 2010a). Interactivity in this context refers to the degree of responsiveness established in a two-way communication multimedia environment. Beauchamp (2010) considers that interactivity plays a fundamental role in promoting learning in England. He cites the Department for Education and Employment (DfEE, 1998), which defines interactivity as the ability to respond contingently to the learner's actions. DfEE (1999) characterises interactivity as one of the factors contributing to success in learning, along with discussion, pace, confidence and ambition.

The analysis of interaction is based on reciprocity (Kirsh, 1997), which requires cooperation. The parties involved must co-ordinate their activity or the process will descend into chaos. All parties exercise power over each other, influencing what the others will do, and there is usually some degree of (tacit) negotiation over who will do what, when and how. Thus, in this respect, interactivity is a complex, dynamic coupling between two or more intelligent parties. In some instances, interaction does not require explicit co-operation, negotiation or coordination; an example of this, given by Kirsch (1997), is the interaction amongst the bodies in the solar system. The moon's gravitational field acts on the Earth and Sun, just as the Earth and the Sun's gravitational fields act on the moon (and all other solar bodies); this occurs mutually and reciprocally, and everything is automatic and axiomatic. Kirsch (1997) also gives an example of intermediate interaction: when someone is bouncing on a trampoline, that person is interacting with it, in the sense that his behaviour is closely coupled with its behaviour and vice-versa. These environments of action, rich with reactive potential, are not agents themselves, capable of forming goals and therefore capable of performing truly reciprocal actions.

The above definition is not the only one found in the literature, and others have attempted to define the term *interactivity* in a way that is closer to this study. For example, Sims (1994; 1992) describes interactivity as a series of seven levels, in which each is distinguished by the form of communication between the user and the computer. Moore (1989) proposed three different types of interactivity: learner-content interaction, learner-instructor interaction, and learner-learner interaction. He described learner-content interaction as a fundamental characteristic of education. Indeed, interaction and interactivity are considered characteristic features of multimedia materials: interaction is present in all components of instructional materials (the content, the organisation and the interface through which it is presented). Furthermore, interaction plays a communicative role in the human-computer dialogue.

From a cognitive perspective, the incorporation of interactivity within computer-based systems rests with the learner's freedom to influence the flow of information, in terms of timing or content. For example, button-clicking can be used to allow the learner to indicate when he or she wants the next portion of text to be displayed, and interactive multiple-choice questions can be used to provide meaningful feedback for self-assessment. In the multimedia environment, interactivity is the key to enhancing learning by supporting higher levels of cognitive activity among students. Evans & Gibbons (2007) emphasised that interactivity is a fundamental mechanism in both knowledge acquisition and the development of cognitive skills; in their research, interactivity encouraged the learner to play an active role in the control of the pace and management of the presented material. These types of interactivity have strong implications for deep learning.

Evans and Sabry (2003) formulated the interaction model in order to study the processes and the effects of interaction in learning. The three-stage model of computer-initiated interactions defines the terminology and methodology as follows: according to the model, an interaction involves a sequence of three actions—initiation, response and feedback, with exchange of information occurring between the two agents involved. In a multimedia system, initiation refers to the system's request for input, in order to begin the process. The response refers to the second agent providing the input, and feedback is the reaction to the first agent's input. The three actions are interrelated, and are a direct consequence of each agent's response. The term *interactivity* thus includes interaction between students (student–student interaction), interaction with the tutor (teacher–student interaction) and interaction with the teaching material itself (student–content interaction) (Moore, 1989; Schrum & Berge, 1997). In their study, Evans and Gibbons (2007) claim that due to an *interactivity effect,* students learn better when they interact with a simulation (in terms of control and pace) and answer interactive self-assessment questions. In Evans and Gibbons' (2007) study, learners interacted with an e-learning system and could control the pace of the presentation by indicating when they were ready to jump to the next part of the presentation.

Evans and Sabry (2003) pointed out that all forms of computer-initiated interactivity may be described in terms of their model, and it has three actions in terms of navigation or pacing interaction:

1. Present button or control to learner (computer initiation);
2. Student presses button or uses control (learner response);
3. Present new information to learner (computer feedback).

A lesson in a computer-based learning system may be described as non-interactive if it requires little or no computer-initiated interactivity in order for a lesson to be completed. In contrast, a computer-based learning system is said to be interactive if it uses computer-initiated interactivity as an intrinsic part of the lesson. Interactivity is examined in general and within the context of the different multimedia principles that underpin the design of research experiments, relating to interactive pedagogical feedback, interactive audio feedback and interactive texting feedback mechanisms.

2.6.1 Interactivity Components

An interesting approach in studying interactivity is to focus on the essential components that must be present in a session of interaction (Zazelenchuk, 1997). The six essential components, with regard to the above, are as follows: active learning environment, learner control, feedback, multiple media, learner response option and adaptability.

Active Learning Environment refers to an educational environment that provides the student with the resources to become actively involved in a learning activity. Zazelenchuk (1997) stated that an interactive learning environment requires learners to actively process the information that is being presented to them by the multimedia programme. Learners will thereby actively engage in analysis, comparing, modifying and other dynamic instructional activities (Wilson, 1999).

Learner Control refers to the opportunity of learners to direct the course of their process of learning (Lawless & Brown, 1997). Lawless & Brown (1997) identified two types of control within the multimedia environment: external (programme control or PC) and internal (learner control or LC). PC refers to the specific limits set up by a multimedia computer program which all users must deal with, and the most common types of LC are pacing and sequencing. Pacing allows learners to specify how much time they want to invest in each of the tasks for the entire lesson, while sequencing allows learners to choose their path, in terms of educational content. Pedagogically speaking, LC is important because individual students learn more when allowed to control their instruction (as opposed to learners without such control) (Hannafin & Sullivan, 1995). However, an overloaded multimedia design may generate a multitude of options and choices available to learners, thus imposing a cognitive load on them (Lim, 2004).

Interactive Feedback is considered as a reactive computer response to learner input. Feedback on learning encompasses a great range of activities that provide diagnoses and remedial suggestions for changing future actions.

Multiple Media or Multimedia refers to the blending of sound, music, images and other media into a synchronized whole. The term is also referred to as cross-media, which means live demonstrations by human speakers, supported by a combination of slide projectors, motion-picture projectors and audio-tape players. Furthermore, the term *digital multimedia* is used to distinguish such multimedia from artistic works, audiovisual presentations, theatre and other non-computer-based multimedia. Interactive multimedia systems enable end users to choose the information they see and receive by actively engaging with the system (Lang, 2006). However, interactivity is not unique to digital media; it has long been a feature of traditional media, such as newspapers, where readers must scan a page and decide what articles to read and in what sequence. For the sake of precision, the term *interactive digital multimedia* is thus preferable to *multimedia* or *interactive multimedia.*

Learner Response Option considers that learners communicate or interact with a computer program by typing, dragging a mouse or joystick, pressing an image on a touch screen, giving a voice command to voice recognition systems or any other associated type of input (Zazelenchuk, 1997). The availability of feedback and learner response options are essential characteristics of interactive systems.

Adaptability refers to the ability of a computer system to adapt to a variety of individual learners' needs (Zazelenchuk, 1997). It is the adaptation of the interaction process and the exchange of information between individuals (Chou, 2003) and it is expected that a computer program should be capable of adapting to the preferred learning style of a particular student and that the computer system must be able to adapt to the learner's needs and reciprocate accordingly.

A further taxonomy (Hannafin, 1989) is based on the classification of the five functions of interaction, which are confirmation, pacing, inquiry, navigation, and elaboration. Interaction is considered as having been achieved if one or more instructional functions are presented and procedural control with cognitive processing effects is provided.

Confirmation verifies that the intended learning has taken place, and typically focuses on the learners' attainment of the intended lesson objectives. Through confirmation, student progress is monitored, branching is executed and decisions are enforced, in terms of activities in subsequent lessons. Typically, criterion-referenced questions are embedded during a lesson, which requires the demonstration of knowledge or skills.

Pacing refers to lesson control through clear directions or indications, such as "click the arrow to proceed". Pacing options optimise learning by taking into account students' reading and processing rates, which differ, and some research has found evidence indicating that students learn better when they are able to control the order and pace of a presentation (Mayer, Dow & Mayer, 2003).

Inquiry increases access to lesson support, based upon uniquely defined needs. Inquiries often take the form of help routines or student-accessible lesson features, such as performance updates and lists of completed lesson sections.

Navigation is concerned with the route of the lesson sections, and interaction provides the learner with controlled access to defined parts of a lesson. Normally, the specific navigational functions are provided via designer-imposed menu options.

Elaboration refers to the process of relating previously successfully encoded knowledge with current lesson content, and this is accomplished through the use of pedagogical strategies such as encouraging the learner to compare and contrast existing knowledge with new lesson content or to combine additional relevant information with current lesson content.

2.6.2 Interactive Multimedia

Multimedia systems are an important key environment of interactivity and such systems use computers to present text, graphics, video, animation and sound in an integrated manner (Domagk et al., 2010). More specifically, multimedia systems deliver content using concurrent types of media communication in one presentation which combines different content forms. A concurrent type of media communication is a CD-ROM, website, etc., and these communication and media technologies are permitted to interactively amalgamate a blend of information built into a variety of content forms, such as text, audio, still images, animation and video. From a technology perspective, it entails the use of multiple forms of delivery device, such as computers, screens and loudspeakers (Olson, 1988). Mayer and Chandler (2001) defined multimedia as words and pictures that provide an account of how a cause-and-effect system works. Multimedia presentations are engaging because they stimulate human senses through a combination of sounds and images.

In a multimedia computer system, interaction may be initiated by the system or by the learner (Schar & Krueger, 2000). When a student initiates interaction, he or she seeks information from the content in a similar way to other traditional media. When interaction is initiated by the system, it demands some input from the learner, such as pressing a button or answering a question. In the case of computer-initiated interaction, the response action is performed by the learner and the feedback action is performed by the computer.

There is evidence that multimedia and interactivity help to convey an instructional message. For example, Mayer (1997; 1998b) carried out various studies in which learners indicated that they understood explanations better when a message was constructed using words and pictures. The use of multimedia can offer a new perspective compared to the traditional static representation of information. Students experience deeper learning from well designed multimedia presentations than from traditional, verbal-only messages (Mayer, 1997; Moreno & Mayer, 1999). However, these multimedia materials should be designed according to a theoretical framework and the principles set out in the following section to deliver the instructional message appropriately.

The theory of multimedia learning (Mayer, 1997) implies that meaningful learning takes place when relevant information in each store is digested into a coherent representation and makes connections between corresponding representations in each store. Web-based multimedia e-learning systems are ideal tools for complementing or replacing the traditional delivery of teaching and e-learning, and may be defined as a combination of technology and the pedagogical approaches required for presenting and teaching a particular subject. e-Learning systems are key delivery components in communicating the educational message through the use of text and visual images. However, the heuristic of using text and visual images is simply one element in a series of design principles whose implementation improves the effectiveness of teaching through the use of web-based multimedia e-learning. The theory of multimedia learning is based on three main assumptions, namely: there are two separate channels (auditory and visual) for the processing of information; there is limited channel capacity; and learning is an active process of filtering, selecting, organising and integrating information (Mayer & Moreno, 1998a; Mayer, 2001; Moreno & Mayer, 1999).

According to Mayer (2001), in the Multimedia Theory of Learning, information is presented in more than one mode (for example, as words or pictures), with all modes facilitating learning. Mayer asserted that meaningful learning occurs when learners mentally select relevant information and build coherent mental connections, and he developed a series of research-based learning techniques in which information is integrated and proportionally distributed into the auditory and visual channels, in order to maximise the learner's working memory, because people learn better when multimedia messages are designed in a way that is consistent with how the human mind works.

The Multimedia Theory of Learning, and specifically the concepts related to the auditory channels are given due consideration in "Chapter Five Interactive Audio Feedback." The study presented in this section investigates whether the speed enhancements of speaking rather than typing are carried over to the process of creating feedback. The results are presented after extensive research has been conducted.

2.6.3 Multimedia Principles

Mayer (2005) devised a series of principles for designing instructional messages within a multimedia environment leading to constructivist learning, which are as follows:

The multimedia or multiple representation principle asserts that it is better to use narration and pictures (two modes) to present an explanation rather than narration or pictures alone (one mode). This multimedia effect is consistent with the cognitive theory of multimedia learning (Mayer & Moreno, 1998a), as those given a multimedia explanation are capable of creating two different mental representations relating to the auditory and visual channels and making connections between them. In Mayer's experiments (Mayer & Anderson, 1992), students who listened to a narration explaining how a bicycle tyre pump works while also viewing a corresponding animation generated twice as many useful solutions to subsequent problem-solving transfer questions as those students who listened to the same narration without viewing any animation.

The coherence principle (Moreno & Mayer, 1999) indicates that students learn better when extraneous material is excluded from multimedia explanations. Based on the cognitive theory of multimedia learning, this is due to limitations in the capacity of the visual and auditory channels. If a narrated multimedia animation presentation is delivered, the narrated component flows through the auditory channel, while the animation is processed by the visual channel. Any additional auditory or visual information competes with its earlier-presented counterpart, with a tendency to overload. Less capacity being available for the processing of narration negatively affects students' learning.

The modality principle recommends the use of narration with pictures rather than written words with pictures. Research by Mayer and Moreno (1998a) showed that when students are listening to verbal information instead of visually witnessing on-screen text, they outperform those who learn through concurrent on-screen text and animations. This group may have an advantage in being able to experience two channel of information simultaneously; i.e., the auditory and the visual channels, while the latter group may overload the visual channel, with two visual sources competing for the same channel.

The spatial and temporal contiguity principles (Moreno & Mayer, 1999) relate to how far display words should be placed away from pictures. The principle is consistent with the cognitive theory of multimedia learning, as corresponding words and pictures must be in working memory at the same time in order to facilitate a connection between them.

The spatial contiguity principle recommends the displaying of words adjacent to the parts of the picture to which they relate. In giving a multimedia explanation, this means presenting corresponding words and pictures contiguously rather than separately. Research has demonstrated that students who learn through integrated verbal and visual explanations outperform those who learn using material that was separated (Mayer, 1997). In a review of ten studies concerning whether multimedia instruction was effective, Mayer (1997) manipulated the physical proximity of the on-screen text and animation, and concluded that there was consistent evidence in favour of what is referred to as the 'spatial-contiguity effect'.

The temporal contiguity principle refers to the fact that students understand an explanation better when corresponding words and pictures are presented at the same time, as opposed to their being shown separately. For example, students who listened to a narration explaining how a bicycle tyre pump works whilst also viewing a corresponding animation outperformed students who viewed the animation before or after listening to the narration (Mayer & Anderson, 1992).

The redundancy principle (Mayer & Moreno, 1998b) recommends the use of narration and pictures rather than narration, text and pictures, providing the visual information is presented simultaneously with the verbal information. There is a misconception that when using a multimedia learning system, the more material presented (such as animations, video, graphics with simultaneous text and audio) the better the message will be delivered. Unfortunately, redundant information presented simultaneously through different channels will only achieve the overloading of the channel due to the split-attention effect (Mayer & Moreno, 1998b; Moreno & Mayer, 1999) of the on-screen text and the animation, and the redundant message hinders rather than assists student learning. However, students presented with redundant verbal material outperformed those students who learned through non-redundant verbal materials when such presentations were sequential.

The split-attention principle (Chandler & Sweller, 1991; Sweller et al., 1990) recommends the presenting of words as auditory narration rather than as visual on-screen text. The rationale for this is that on-screen text and animation can overload the visual information processing system, whereas narration is processed in the verbal information processing system and animation is processed in the visual information processing system. For example, students who viewed an animation while also listening to a corresponding narration outperformed students who viewed the same animation with corresponding on-screen text consisting of the same words as the narration.

The personalisation principle (Kartal, 2010) states that using words in a conversational style rather than a formal style increases learning. The conversational style aids learning because people work harder to understand material when they feel they are in conversation with a partner. In the formal style, the first and second-person narrative is avoided.

The segmenting material principle recommends that learning material is presented in learner-paced segments rather than as a continuous unit (Mayer, 2005). Students learn more deeply when a multimedia message is presented in user-paced segments rather than as a continuous unit and segmenting slows the pace of the presentation, enabling the learner to carry out essential mental processing.

The pre-training learning principle recommends that it is better if learners are familiar with the names and characteristics of the main concepts (Clark & Mayer, 2003). This equips students with knowledge that can be used to process the next multimedia message with less cognitive effort.

The signalling principle recommends that it is preferable that words include cues in the organisation of a presentation (Mayer, 2005). The learner's attention is held by highlighting or flashing the appropriate elements in the multimedia message, and this helps to reduce extraneous cognitive load within the learning process.

The voice principle recommends that it is better if words are spoken in a standard-accent by a human (Mayer, 2005). People learn more deeply from a multimedia message when the narration is done by a human rather than by a computerised voice. The human voice triggers a social response in the learner that encourages him or her to make sense of the information presented.

The image principle indicates that learning performance is improved when the speaker's image is added to the screen.

The individual differences principle indicates that multimedia effects, contiguity effects and split-attention create the largest effect on high spatial or low knowledge learners and are dependent on individual differences in the learners. For example, students with greater prior knowledge may not require a contiguous visual presentation because they can generate their own mental images while listening to an animation or reading a verbal text. In addition, students who score high on spatial ability tests show greater multimedia effects than those students who score low on spatial ability. In accordance with the cognitive theory of multimedia learning, students with greater spatial ability are able to hold the visual image in visual working memory and so are more likely to benefit from the contiguous presentation of words and pictures. For example, students who lack prior knowledge are inclined to show stronger multimedia effects and contiguity effects than those students who possess high levels of prior knowledge (Mayer & Gallini, 1990). The eleven principles presented above encompass the cognitive theory of multimedia learning.

2.7 Practice

Traditional practice is defined as asking questions during instruction, and evidence has been provided that adjunct questions increase the amount learned from a written passage (Rothkopf, 1966). Other researchers (Hannafin, Phillips & Tripp, 1986; Hannafin et al., 1987; Salisbury, 1988) have studied this instructional variable in depth in order to consider its importance in increasing learning. Learning is believed to be the result of the frequent rehearsal of relevant lesson information paired with appropriate feedback and reinforcement (Wager & Wager, 1985), and although such behavioural practice activities are believed to be most effective for lower level or fact learning, interactive approaches and new pedagogical designs elicit cognitive and deeper learning.

In this realm, Rieber (1990) considered two types of practice (behavioural and cognitive) that integrate with our general theories in order to explain how learning occurs. Behavioural practice, with a large reinforcing component of practice activity, consisted of five multiple-choice questions, presented after each of the four lesson parts in Rieber's research. The questions covered the relevant material in each lesson part, with feedback provided to the students in the form of information on the correct results. Rieber's (1990) experiment consisted of a structured simulation activity in which students were given increasing levels of control over an interactive dynamic that simulated a free-floating object in a frictionless, gravity-free environment. The free-floating object was called a *starship*, and was represented by a triangular symbol on the computer screen. Students practiced increasing and decreasing the speed of the starship after the third part of the lesson, and after the fourth part of the lesson they applied forces to the starship in 90° increments, which demonstrated how orthogonal forces affect the starship's trajectory in two-dimensional space. The experiment focused on cognitive practice.

2.8 Assessment

Assessment may be a frightening and threatening experience for teachers and students alike (Gibbs, 1999). Technological innovations triggered by computer and network-based learning have given assessment a new dimension and changed this emotional and highly sensitive activity. The core of these innovations is interactivity and its intrinsic features to produce an instant or repetitive response (DfEE, 1998). With technology-driven education over recent decades, teachers are focusing more on assessment for learning in which the role of the learner changed from passive to active. Therefore, the role of the teachers transforms from a dominant to a flexible position where their actions facilitate comprehension of ideas built on learners' own cognitive conceptions. Thus, Interactivity becomes a tool in the hands of the teachers to adapt and/or enable their assessment pedagogies. It also provides the learner with an instant mechanism to test the understanding of the educational resources.

Assessment is generally considered a term that involves the process of giving students tests and then assigning grades to them. More specifically, it is a mechanism for providing either the teachers (summative assessment) or the learners (formative assessment) with vital information for improving their teaching/learning methodology and determining (if accompanied by feedback) where mistakes have been made, to reflect on them and become more effective, self-assessing, self-directed learners (Angelo & Cross, 1993).

Assessment has long been categorised depending on whether the purpose of the evaluation is summative or formative (Black & William, 1998; Boud, 1995; Bransford, Brown & Cocking, 2000; Brown & Knight, 1994; Buchanan, 2000; Khan, Davies & Gupta, 2001; Manogue et al., 2002; Velan et al., 2002). The former measures performance during or at the end of a lesson, unit of study, etc., while formative assessment plays an important role in an assessment-centred learning environment, motivating students to learn and directing their learning (Bransford et al., 2000) and improving their knowledge and skills (Morss & Murray, 2005).

Assessment is one of the most important topics for future research into the effect of interactivity because it is an area for measuring learning outcomes performance. Therefore, it plays an important role in all the sections of the research conducted in this book that evaluate learner performance. It is also an important function of formative assessment to provide students with "meaningful feedback" that should occur continuously, but not intrusively, as part of instruction. In addition, this is beneficial in the adjustment of teaching strategies and in the application of appropriate remedial techniques. Research (Bell & Cowie, 2001) has suggested that the teacher should gather formative assessment information (feedback) from student learning activities and then respond to promote further learning.

Formative assessment refers to the help provided to the learner, in order to improve their knowledge and skills (Morss & Murray, 2005). With the advent of technology-driven education over the past decades, teachers are focusing more on assessment for learning in which the role of the learner changes from passive to active. The role of the teacher is thus transformed from a dominant to a flexible position; they act to facilitate the comprehension of ideas built upon the learners' own cognitive conceptions. Self-assessment provides the pertinent mechanism for enhancing individual performance, either through summative or formative evaluation, and is used in courses within the medical profession that implement CPD (continuing professional development) activities to disseminate expertise and in staff development that is self-directed and electronically delivered (Dorman, 2008).

Activities that contribute to assessment for learning include the use of detailed feedback, teacher questioning, and built-in specific learning goals and self-assessment. In this context, self-assessment is formative assessment, which provides feedback for reflection on learning activities.

2.8.1 Self-Assessment

Self-assessment provides a pertinent mechanism for enhancing individual performance, either through summative or formative evaluation. It generates feedback for learners through reflection on learning activities. It is used in courses within the medical profession that implement CPD (continuing professional development) activities to disseminate their expertise and for staff development that is self-directed and electronically delivered (Dorman, 2008).

2.8.2 Interactive Self-Assessment Questions

Interactivity is examined within the context of the different multimedia principles that underpin the design of research experiments related to interactive pedagogical feedback using interactive self-assessment questions (ISAQ) . Interactivity plays a pivotal role in all scenarios, but its importance is highlighted when used as part of an ISAQ. An ISAQ is a computer-based multiple-choice or text-entry question that requires input from the learner and provides feedback based on that input (Evans & Gibbons, 2007). Self-assessment provides the pertinent mechanism for enhancing individual performance: it is a type of formative assessment that provides feedback to learners, so that they may reflect upon learning activities. Interactive self-assessment questions, if they are to be effective, must be designed using well-established design principles. These principles, when applied to the design of the web-learning content, create the playground for the fostering of deep learning, where interactivity plays a crucial role in student education. Research on the interactivity effect (Evans & Gibbons, 2007; Mayer, 2001) has indicated that learner performance increases when students are exposed to a system which interactively reacts to their input through self-assessment questions.

However, in order to work effectively, the technology must be embraced within pedagogical methods, in order to elicit performance and provide a well guided element of interactivity. Interactive self-assessment questions, if they are to be effective, must be designed in accordance with well-established design principles (Mayer, 2001). These principles, when applied to the design of web-learning content, create the potential to foster deep learning wherever interactivity play a crucial role in student education (Evans & Sabry, 2003).

A basic characteristic of interactivity is learner control of the pace of a multimedia presentation, which establishes that students learn better when they are allowed to control the flow of the presentation or a narrated animation (Mayer & Chandler, 2001). Studies that allow students the freedom to interact and control their own pace while learning in a computer-based simulation show evidence of higher performance (Mayer et al., 2003), while research on the interactivity effect has indicated that learner performance increases when they are exposed to a system that interactively reacts to their input through self-assessment questions (Evans & Gibbons, 2007). ISAQ have the potential to indicate to what extent a user's response is correct or incorrect; they thus allow the learner to actively engage in the presented material, in order to build cognitive mental representations. Examples can be seen at Chapter Four Interactive Pedagogical Feedback. ISAQ are designed and introduced in academic lessons in this section to study their effects.

2.9 Feedback

It is important to refresh the understanding and role of this concept, since an ISAQ is a mechanism for providing feedback. Feedback in a broad perspective is the process used to help learners indicate where and how their learning experience can be improved, and has long been recognised as an important instrument in the improvement of education (Smit et al., 2008). Feedback on learning encompasses a great range of activities that provide a diagnosis and remedial suggestions for changing future actions. Feedback can make students more effective, self-assessing, self-directed learners, and is usually related to assessment as a constructive response to coursework and exams. However, high-quality individualised and meaningful feedback is expensive to provide: it also takes time to design and implement (World Economic Forum, 2002), as research by the Open University has demonstrated. However, it compensates for this effort by actively engaging the learner and increasing the depth of the student's understanding, in terms of increased performance in problem-solving transfer questions (Evans & Gibbons, 2007). The effectiveness of feedback in improving learning has made its implementation valuable (Gibbs, 2003) and various implementations have been used to maintain or increase these positive effects, while diminishing the burden on cost and workload. For example, Gibbs (2003) outlined a two-stage test, used in medicine, which incorporates both formative and summative assessments. In the first test, formative assessment is only used to inform the students, grab their attention and present remedial feedback that provides a diagnosis and remedial suggestions for the changing of future actions. The second test, in the same topic area, comes two weeks later and implements the summative assessment only, giving marks but no feedback, in order to determine what has been learnt.

Many educators recognize the crucial role that feedback plays in contributing to the learning process (Kumar & Stracke, 2011; Wang & Wu, 2008). Recently, the effectiveness of formal feedback has undergone some scrutiny. For example, Søndergaard and Thomas (2004) found that in a survey implemented in their faculty, one in three students disagreed or strongly disagreed with the statement: "I received helpful feedback on how I was going". They argue that this dissatisfaction is widespread. There is also a growing body of evidence that indicates that the potential benefits of feedback are often not attained (Chanock, 2000; Duncan, 2007; Hounsell et al., 2008). There is recognition amongst authors that providing feedback is often a time consuming activity, and that if the feedback system is to be improved it must not increase the workload of tutors. Clearly, if learners are to benefit from feedback it must be relatively quick and easy for tutors to provide it to an adequate standard.

2.10 Audio Feedback

Another type of feedback manipulated in this research is audio feedback. Whilst written or typewritten feedback seems to be the norm, there is evidence to suggest that spoken feedback is much more easily generated. Developmental studies indicate that written skills develop much later than oral skills and take more cognitive processing to exercise (Grabowski, 2010), and this cognitive overhead may partially explain why most people find it quicker to speak than to write. This suggests that one mechanism for reducing the workload burden for creating feedback might be to use the spoken rather than the written modality.

Several studies have considered the relative speeds of speaking and writing. In early informal studies, Gould (1978) suggested that people could handwrite memorised material at about 40 words per minute (wpm), but speak it or read aloud at around 200 wpm. Card (1983) reported that an experienced typist could reach approximately 80 wpm. Of course, the process of generating feedback is not simply a matter of speaking or writing; it also involves the critical evaluation of students' work and the synthesis of sentences. The real test is whether the speed enhancements of speaking rather than typing carry over to the process of creating feedback.

2.11 Audience Response System

Audience response systems (ARS) have followed the traditional trial and error path in their evolution (Kay & LeSage, 2009). They were initially introduced at Stanford University in 1966, and featured as an expensive piece of technology that did not function as expected. ARS became commercially available from 1992 to 1999, but cost was still a limitation in widespread distribution. They were substantially in use from 2003, due to affordability and technology reasons.

ARS technology is considered an excellent tool in creating further interactivity and engagement within the classroom (Collins, 2006). Learning is underpinned through the provision of immediate feedback, focusing students' attention, identifying any gaps in knowledge and enhancing student involvement. There is great agreement that the ARS promote learning when coupled with appropriate pedagogical methodologies (Fies & Marshall, 2006) (e.g., TEFA) (Beatty & Gerace, 2009). It can also be used as a mediated tool in overcoming the limitations imposed by the traditional methods of education. The loss of attention is apparent after prolonged periods of teaching, with only 25 per cent of students recalling material during a 3 hour, one-way lecture (McIntosh, 1996).

ARS is the integration of hardware and software and allows the lecturer to pose real-time questions to students. The students reply with an answer using different types of handheld devices, e.g. clickers (TurningPoint, 2007) (Figure 4), laptops, personal digital assistants and mobile phones (Beatty & Gerace, 2009). After responses are received, the software compiles and displays the results using histograms or percentage graphs (Collins, 2006).

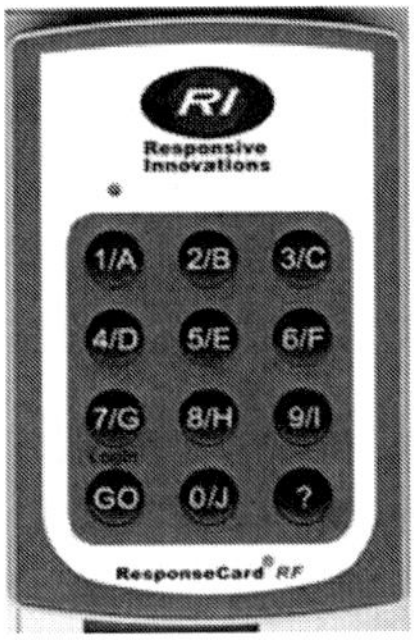

Figure 3: The Turning Point Clicker (TurningPoint, 2007)

There are obvious benefits to using the ARS system. Indeed, Robin's (2009) comprehensive review of 67 peer-reviewed papers from 2000 to 2007 highlighted the benefits and challenges associated with the use of an ARS. The relevant benefits within the classroom environment included improved attendance, an increase in the levels of attention and participation and the intensification of engagement: students are more interested in the concepts presented and discussed through an ARS. In addition, audio response systems enhance the learning experience as a result of their interactive characteristics, the quantity and quality of class discussions, teaching guidance, improvements in performance and the quality of education.

A key beneficial element of ARS is within the field of assessment. General feedback and feedback in the form of formative assessment is used to determine students' understanding of concepts, thus helping to identify misconceptions that may alter the course of classroom instruction (Bergtrom, 2006; Jackson et al., 2005; Siau, Sheng & Nah, 2006).

2.12 Short Message Services (SMS)

Short Message Services (SMS) are an active part of Chapter Six Interactive Texting Feedback. SMS enables mobile phones to receive and send text messages through a network operator's message centre or from the Internet through "SMS gateway" websites (Lai, 2004). SMS messages are transmitted to a subscriber's mobile number via an SMSC (Short Message Service Centre). SMSCs are not restricted to sending SMS just to the subscribers of the mobile network the SMSC belongs to, they can send to any international mobile subscriber that the mobile network, or its backbone provider, has interworking or roaming agreements with.

SMS is an almost instantaneous communication medium when compared to the conventional email because of the differences in the concept of operation. SMS operates on a 'store-and-forward' concept (even if the recipient's phone is switched off, they will still be able to receive the message) while email operates on a 'store-and-retrieve' concept (senders must wait for the receiver to come on-line and access the network to retrieve the message).

2.13 e-Learning Systems

Technology has propelled an evolution of distance learning in the last forty years that has generated a confusing variety of terms (Morabito, Sack, and Bhate; 1999). Blended, distance, online and e-learning are concepts that portray learning in different combination with technology. Blended learning, for example mixes e-learning with traditional teaching and learning practices. Typically, there is a combination of classroom teaching interaction with online learning. Distance learning gives the learners the opportunity to study at their own pace and place separating learning from the tutor. Therefore, there is no requirement for attendance at a campus-based organization. Online learning describes learning that takes place in a network environment and usually requires connection to the Internet. e-learning (the subject of this research) relates to the appropriate use of Information and Communication Technologies(ICT) to enhance the learning in any of these contexts. Therefore, it can take place in a campus-based organization or any other context. ICT as a particular mechanism for delivering educational resources has a huge potential for enhancing learning that has not been unveiled yet. Although interactivity is present in all these types of activities this research is limited to the effect of interactivity on e-learning systems to narrow the scope.

e-Learning is defined as "learning facilitated and supported through the use of information and communications technology" (Knight, 2007). Indeed, e-learning is considered a significant internet service, due to the increasing dissemination of knowledge (Carchiolo et al., 2007) and its widespread use in higher education (Lu & Chiou, 2010). Its increasing popularity is a response to the benefits produced. Such benefits in the use of e-learning systems are that they can be used at any time and in any place, allow the creation of learning communities, and facilitate the implementation of a learner-centred approach that helps deal with the many differences between learners (Lu & Chiou, 2010).

Although research comparing the effectiveness of educational television and face-to-face instruction found little difference in student achievement (Wetzel, Radtke & Stem, 1994), and a distance learning study (Storck & Sproull, 1995) found no differences between the performance of students given interactive video instruction and face-to-face instruction, advances in technology have indicated that more interactive teaching styles are positively associated with the effectiveness of learning outcomes (Webster & Hackley, 1997). Effectiveness is an important indicator of an effective learning management system (LMS), as presented in Douglas's (2004) research. The results of his research indicated that student performance is significantly improved by the incorporation of multiple choices within the e-learning environment.

2.14 Learning Objects

Learning objects were used as components of the e-learning systems considered in Chapter Four Interactive Pedagogical Feedback. The research doesn't revolve around its features, but centres more specifically on an open learning approach as described by Lewis (1986). The approach "enables people to learn at the time, place and pace which satisfy their circumstances and requirements".

Learning objects were used to provide precise content in the lessons designed in this research. A Learning Object (LO) is defined (Fig. 4) as a re-usable self-contained digital entity with embedded metadata resources and a learning strategy that may interact with other objects and encapsulate other resources (information instances) in an interconnected and platform independent environment (Palacios, 2002). It is tagged with metadata based on the SCORM standard, in order to describe the elements of content (Palacios, 2008).

The general term Information Object (IO) is used to represent several real entities (or groups) with similar properties, rather than one individual. Learning strategies are the methods that students use to learn and/or the pedagogy teachers employ to convey a particular lesson. These range from techniques for improved memory, better study skills and an institutional curriculum designed for a specific course of academic study.

In general, a learning strategy helps to implement methods and adopt techniques that increase effectiveness in any aspect of the general cognitive process of acquiring skills or knowledge. Granularity and reusability properties are essential parts of the learning object concept, and by looking at Figure 4 it may be noted that LOs differ from IOs, because information can be communicated without the intention to teach.

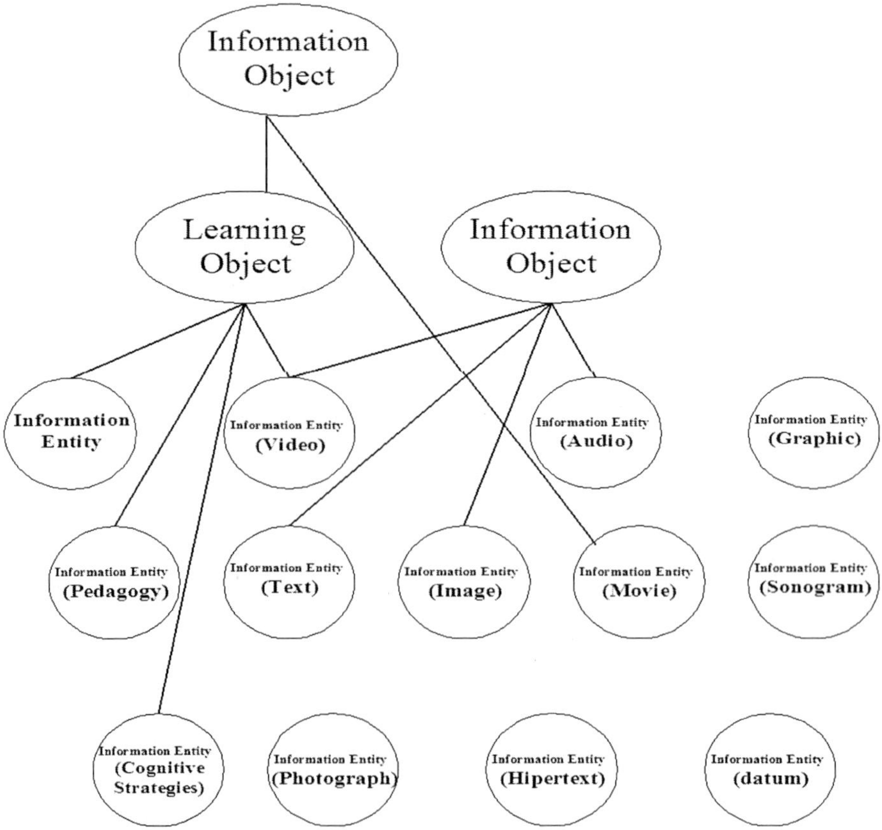

Figure 4: Learning Object as Part of an InfOb Layout (Palacios, 2002a)

Learning repositories should be designed in such a way that the content will be actively used by teachers. The quality of the content is paramount and is retained in the peer evaluation process (Jones & McNaught, 2011).

There are similar systems based on web-based multimedia interactive components, such as the Telelearning system (MITS) (Megzari, Yuan & Karmouch, 2002). This system provides a multimedia interactive learning environment, with easy-to-search and highly reusable learning objects and an emphasis on metadata and media content management mechanisms. Metadata and media contents are generated, stored and utilised in order to facilitate the search and the on-demand presentation of learning objects. Learner preferences, performance and progress information are maintained by the profile database, in order to ensure that courseware presentation is adaptable and more interactive.

2.15 Chapter Discussion

People have the intuitive feeling that technology and interactivity as an intrinsic element improves learning (Conole et al., 2004). A large amount of research on e-learning, for example, claims to derive from well-established theoretical approaches as described at the beginning of the chapter, e.g., cognitivism, constructivism, etc., but no scientific explanation is given for adopting the principles of these approaches in such different contexts. In many cases, there is little scientific evidence that supports these claims. Instructional design underpinned by such flaw perception therefore reflects 'common sense' rather than theoretically informed design.

Using technology to enhance learning requires a more consistent and innovative approach that interrelates the theoretical framework with a scientific methodology that generates the evidence to support such an endeavour (Conole & Oliver, 2002). Conole (2004), for example, amalgamates this conception in her research. Her work intends joining theory and practice using learning design decision-making resources that use a model of pedagogical approaches as a basis for developing effective learning design plans.

Some limitations are perceived to exist when researching the effect of interactivity; an approach that intertwines the theoretical framework with a scientific methodology is therefore taken into consideration to support the findings. Media researchers consider that e-learning creates a new realm for innovative instructional methods to be implemented (Clark, 2001). e-Learning delivery mechanisms (e.g. computer, electronic devices, etc.) have deeply revolutionised present society to the extent of displacing other traditional delivery media, such as the books in this task. However, the delivery mechanism *per se* does not yield learning, but the instructional methods effectively managed by the teacher. Others researchers have found that effective learning remains constant when the same instructional methods are used, but the delivery mechanism has been changed (Mayer, 2001). Therefore, the same pedagogical principles that yield learning in traditional environments are likely to promote learning in electronic environments. However, new instructional designs applied in these new environments that have the potential to enhance learning and promote better learning opportunities need to be supported by scientific methodology. A scientific methodology is a key element to understanding how people learn in an electronic environment (e-Learning). Mayer (2003) points out that three elements are essential for the science of e-learning. The three elements are evidence, theory and applications.

Evidence is "the available body of facts or information indicating whether a belief or proposition is true or valid" (Oxford Dictionaries, 2010). The template of replicated findings originated in precise research (Webler et al., 1991). These factual events can be recreated again and again with similar results. There is a lack of evidence and conceptual framework when investigating the effect of interactivity in e-learning systems that this research intends to deal with.

Three specific scenarios provide the environment to validate the effects of interactivity on e-learning systems. The former scenario relates to Interactive pedagogical feedback that evaluates the effect that different levels of interactivity impinge on the memory and understanding of the students. A chapter in the book "Cases on Transnational Learning and Technologically Enabled Environments" (Palacios & Evans, 2010a) and a journal publication (Palacios & Evans, 2011) are published to support the research. The next study refers to Interactive Audio Feedback. The experimental results were presented with the title "Using Audio to Enhance Learner Feedback" in the International Conference on Education and Management Technology (ICEMT 2011) in Cairo, Egypt. Audio feedback significantly reduces the time used by tutors to produce the required feedback compared to typed text and open an interactive mechanism to channel teachers' emotions and perceptions. The latter scenario is Interactive Texting Feedback that combines technological and pedagogical strategies to improve the learning experience. This scenario underpinned by research was presented in the International Conference on Computer Science and Information Systems 2011 (IADIS 2011) in Rome, with the title "Interactive Feedback in the Classroom using SMS messages". The interactivity effect (replicated findings) is found in a variety of contexts and with a variety of learners in these scenarios.

A theory to support the research on how people learn using e-learning systems that generates testable predictions is another essential element for the science of e-learning. The research shows evidence of an interactivity effect for deep learning (understanding) as indicated both by improvement in transfer test scores and reduced time needed to complete transfer test questions. The weaker effect for memory compared with understanding is consistent with previous multimedia learning studies (summarised in Mayer, 2001) which suggest that effects are more pronounced in transfer tests than in retention tests.

Finally, **the applications** of theory-based principles on how to design electronic learning environments that can be successfully tested in research studies will provide tangible support for the science of e-learning.

This study of interactivity as a vital component of e-learning contributes to the strength the science of e-learning and provides sound evidence. The research experimental hypotheses that follow contribute to providing that evidence. They are also related to the specific learning theories indicated at the beginning of this literature review.

The first study (Chapter Four Interactive Pedagogical Feedback) tests the first hypothesis, that interactivity incorporated in a computer-based system in the form of interactive formative feedback enhances learning. Experimental design manipulating interactivity (with and without the interactive condition) was utilized. Scores were taken from the groups randomly selected to compare differences in performance between the two conditions. This allowed observing the interactivity's effect in the system embedded with ISAQ condition and compare it to the control group. Two types of learning are further examined within the ISAQ condition: recall and transfer. The study takes into consideration mainly cognitive and constructive theories approaches as indicated in section 2.3 above.

The following study (Chapter Five Interactive Audio Feedback) examines interactive audio feedback to evaluate the hypotheses that the process of creating interactive feedback in an audio form is quicker than creating feedback in a typewritten form, and that feedback received in audio form is better quality than feedback received in written form. A mixed method approach was implemented in this study by measuring the performance when using two different condition types (writing and oral). Then, surveys were applied to capture the opinion of the students and lecturers involved in the experiments. The experiments were repeated following an action research methodology as indicated in section 3.2. This study revolt around multimedia theory of learning, dual-coding theory and cognitive theories approaches.

The final study (Chapter Six Interactive Texting Feedback) investigates the hypothesis that interactive texting feedback is an effective approach to enhance learning by implementing a learning environment using an audience response system developed with learner mobiles phones and free website that manage and display learner responses. Construction and generation of knowledge based in previous experience is relevant to this methodology approach. Thus, a constructivism theory, as mentioned in section 2.4 above supports this study.

CHAPTER THREE

RESEARCH METHODOLOGY

3.1 Introduction

As indicated in previous chapters, the research in this book is underpinned by three empirical studies developed following a range of methods explained in detail within the following chapters related. This chapter focuses in presenting an epistemological view that amalgamates and upholds the research to effectively show reliability in the experiments drawn.

The three main research studies developed to support the research hypotheses were conducted either on a framework of positivism or interpretivism (e.g. action research) paradigms. Although positivism and interpretivism paradigms reflect strong specific perspectives to do research, this research is guided by the positivism paradigm, but using a mixed methodology. They are unique experiments that may stand alone to validate specific experimental hypotheses. A mixed approach was therefore considered the more viable methodology to compile and undertake the task that upholds the research hypotheses.

The empirical methodology adopted follows the footsteps of other renowned researchers in the field (Mayer, 2001, 2005; Evans & Gibbons, 2007, and others) who adopted an evidence-based approach in this area of educational research subjective by nature.

The cyclical nature of the action research approach explained in the following section is developed in "Chapter Five Interactive Audio Feedback" for its intrinsic capacity to support new models and research dealing with innovation.

The experiments and methods used in the three studies are then presented in a general manner to provide a glimpse of the details provided in each chapter that follows.

3.2 Methodology

The convergence of research in ICT and a number of other fields and disciplines creates an epistemological challenge. In particular, the knowledge explosion as a result of emerging technologies represents an obstacle to researchers' abilities for processing this high volume of new information (Adair & Vohra, 2003).

The challenge increases with the complexity of social systems, which translates into diverse issues of scientific methodology. The rules applied to scientific events, and their consequent analysis and interpretation, differ from the methodology applied to social phenomena. The need therefore exists for developing and implementing theories or models to better interpret these social events. An integrated methodology thus fits more appropriately to the purpose and amalgamation of the whole study.

Positivism, for example, establishes that educational researchers should "eliminate their biases, remain emotionally uninvolved with the objects of study, and test or empirically justify their stated hypotheses" (Johnson & Onwuegbuzie, 2004). Prevailing academic research is based on positivist epistemology, which considers theory above practice (Reeves, 2002). Research in this context focuses on the development of perdurable theories and principles that underpin the work of practitioners. The positivist scientific approach works well with the exact sciences where predictions and knowledge verification are possible by measurement, experiment, observation and rigorous logical arguments; it has not been very successful in the social sciences, particularly in education.

Positivism is a philosophical ideology with different variants that branch into radical, empirical, logical positivism, etc., which perceives the world as external and objective reality (Miller, 1999). Reality is perceived as a whole entity that can be studied and understood by dividing its constituent parts. Introspective and intuitive knowledge is rejected. The term 'positivism' was first formulated by the nineteenth century French philosopher Auguste Comte. Comte's central idea was that all real knowledge results from experience. Comte's Positivism evolved into Logical Positivism, where metaphysical speculation and views of the world are rejected. Logical positivism applies logic as a mechanism to interpret statements and propositions. Positivism in the social sciences is usually characterized by quantitative approaches.

Critiques of Logical Positivism by Karl Popper, Willard Van Orman Quine and Thomas Kuhn, etc., laid the foundation of post-positivism. Popper's ideas, for example, separate from logical positivism by changing the emphasis from what is verifiable to what is refutable (Halfpenny,

1982). Positivists in their general approach to research are seeking to deduce cause and effect relationships to predict patterns of behaviour. The research purpose is therefore likely to be causal or predictive rather than exploratory. The quantitative researcher then develops a theory and uses this to explore the world. This theoretical framework identifies key variables and their relationships and associations. Valid knowledge is thus derived from following the scientific procedure and considered the source of all authoritative knowledge. Verified data is known as empirical evidence. This view, when applied to both the social and natural sciences holds that society operates according to general laws like the physical world.

Interpretivism, on the other hand, claims for the superiority of constructivism, idealism, relativism, and humanism approaches that proclaim understanding the meaning of knowledge by personal interpretation of it (Schwandt, 1994).

Reeves (2002) is emphatic in proposing that research on ICT technologies applied to the field of education, also referred to in broader terms as "Educational Informatics" by Levy (2003) and "Instructional Technology" by Seels and Richey (1994), must be seen as development research focused on a personal attempt to understand, improve and reform practice. In other words, they consider interpretivism to be a more appropriate approach to understanding and developing research in education. Action research as an interpretivism methodology provides educationalists and practitioners developing online learning materials with a methodology to combine theory with practice. Kemmis and McTaggart (1998) defined action research methodology as a "form of collective, self-reflective inquiry undertaken by participants in social situations in order to improve the rationality and justice of their own social or educational practices, as well as their understanding of these practices and the situations in which these practices are carried out".

This methodology is highly suitable to the development of online learning material where new models and attitudes are required to deal with constantly emerging and evolving environments and interactions. Action research bases a researcher's involvement directly in the configuration and activities themselves. This involvement provides empirical and research evidence, thus allowing for a better understanding and learning of the researcher's own practice by means of investigating and testing different points of view within ad hoc situations, and reacting to the feedback responses. It is a systematic and collaborative collection of evidence to support group reflections. In other words, action research is motivated by the desire to improve the environment by changing it and learning how to improve on it by studying the effects of the changes made. The cornerstone of action research is the collection of feedback from the people (academics, technologists, tutors, administrators, etc.) involved in the activities prior to, during, and after the development of the online resources, in order to adapt solutions to specific teaching and learning needs.

There are many models of action research used by practitioners and adapted to specific educational contexts. Altrichter and Gstettner (1993) proposed a four stage model: (1) finding the starting point for the research; (2) clarifying and expressing the problem; (3) developing and implementing action strategies; and (4) disseminating the acquired knowledge. This framework, although considered generic by its critics, is clear and consistent with basic action research methodologies. Cohen et al. (2000) present a more comprehensive educational model that consists of eight stages: (1) identification, evaluation and formulation of the study; (2) discussion, negotiation and establishing the research question involving all stakeholders; (3) literature review; (4) revision and redefinition of the research question and establishing specific objectives or testable hypotheses; (5) selection of research procedures (i.e. words, data collection methods, teaching methods, etc.); (6) selection of evaluation procedures; (7) implementation of the research design; (8) interpretation of data, and overall evaluation and extension of theory. This generic framework provides a more accurate structure for examining educational settings. However, there is a disadvantage in the model in that there is a lack of links to pedagogical, institutional, and administrative events that might constrain the research.

Amongst educational models, one particularly addresses issues in the realm of online learning with a focus on innovation. The model is entitled "The Educational Management Action Research Model" (EMAR), and it provides, in addition to communication channels to the pedagogical, institutional and other constraining factor areas, the structure and spiral cycles of an action research approach (McPherson & Nunes, 2004). The EMAR model (Fig. 5) was produced as a result of research conducted at the University of Sheffield. It is composed of four basic areas through which a developer interacts by means of four essential cycles that constitute the action research framework (Coghlan & Brannick, 2001). The spiral cycles start with an earlier step, which is essential for the action research to be effective, called Diagnosis. Diagnosis includes data collection, analysis and representations. It is followed by Action Planning that comprises building the curriculum design according to the organisational context and pedagogical model. Action Taking follows, which encompasses instructional design and implementing mechanisms for delivery. And finally Action Evaluation where evaluation is performed on the learning activities, modules and programmes planned.

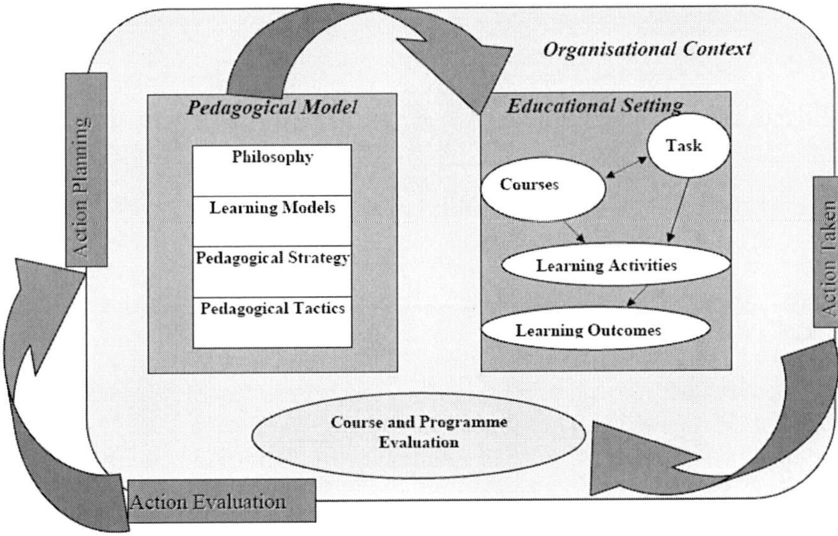

Figure 5: The EMAR Model (Mcpherson and Nunes,2004)

The cycle is repeated at other stages of implementation as a result of feedback collected from learners, subject experts, administrators, technologists, etc. in the previous cycle. There is therefore a continuous process of improvement and refinement before, during and after the development activities. The four basic EMAR areas are: the Organisational Context (OC), the Pedagogical Model (PM), the Educational Setting (ES) and the Evaluation (E) process. It is in these areas that the cycles intersect and they are usually present in any project developing online learning. The OC context, for example, is the engine that drives forward the educational programme while at the same time establishing policies and strategies that constrain its normal flow. The PM introduces the theoretical knowledge that underpins the creation of the learning tasks, activities and outcomes to be implemented, as well as identifying the ICT technologies most appropriate for the delivery and composition of the educational resources. The PM is the place where learning and cognition theories are incorporated into the design. Academic learning involves the acquisition of high level skills of critical thinking and problem solving (McPherson & Nunes, 2004). The ES relates to the curriculum design process by establishing the objectives, content to be delivered and assessment procedures. The ES is the area where the subject expert introduces the syllabus, the specific nature of the content and the ways in which it should be taught. Finally, the most important part of action research is E. E differs from assessment in that the former focuses on examining the holistic nature of the process while the latter focuses particularly on the content. Assessment is therefore more related to the programme and the efficiency in achieving the learning outcomes. Evaluation is intended to monitor all the activities related to the learning process, and provide useful feedback and remedial actions.

Both philosophical approaches attempt to provide warranted assertions about a particular problem or social phenomenon (Biesta & Burbules, 2003). Both approaches describe their data, look for valid explanation from their data, and speculate about the reasons the outcomes they observed occurred (Sechrest and Sidani, 1995). Tensions between advocates of quantitative and qualitative research paradigms have engaged in a passionate dispute. Mixed methods research (mixed research is a synonym) considered a natural complement to traditional qualitative and quantitative research represents a third paradigm to be taken into account as an alternative to the traditional research paradigms (Johnson & Onwuegbuzie, 2004).

Mixed methods research based on methodological pluralism guided the implementation of a mixed approach to sustain the structure and amalgamate this research. Educational research deals with the complexity of social systems that cannot easily be reduced, even for study reasons. Gill and Johnson (1997) suggest that "methodological pluralism" is the most appropriate approach to undertaking studies developed in social systems.

Mixed methods research doesn't intend to resolve the metaphysical, epistemological, and methodological differences between advocates of quantitative and qualitative research paradigms, but attempts to amalgamate the insights provided by qualitative and quantitative research into a balanced solution underpinned by the pragmatic method of classical pragmatists as Charles Sanders Peirce, William James, and John Dewey (Johnson & Onwuegbuzie, 2004). In this regard, research approaches should be mixed in such a way that provides the best opportunities for answering important research questions. The pragmatic rule states that the current meaning of an expression is to be determined by the experiences or practical consequences of belief in or use of the expression in the world (Murphy, 1990). This outcome-orientated rule can be applied through thinking (thinking about what will happen if you do X). Neither Quantitative (empirical evidence) nor Qualitative data provide an answer to all research questions. Mixed methods research empowers the problem situation to decide the appropriate methodology (Niaz, 2008).

In addition to the statement about the research approaches followed in this book previously described, sample size constitutes a fundamental element for generalization (Wiersma & Jurs, 2005). The sample size as an important feature of any empirical study allows inferences about a population to be made (Lindquist, 1940).

In summary, traditional positivism research focuses on deduction, confirmation, theory/hypothesis testing, explanation, prediction, standardized data collection, and statistical analysis. Traditional interpretivism research is concerned with induction, discovery, exploration, theory/hypothesis generation, the researcher as the primary "instrument" of data collection, and qualitative analysis.

On the other hand, the major characteristics of action research are better understanding, participation, improvement, reform, problem finding, problem solving, a step-by-step process, modification, and theory building.

To be effective, a mixed research approach should consider the relevant characteristics of each approach in such a way as to determine when and how their strengths are complemented, and that there their weaknesses do not overlap (Johnson & Onwuegbuzie, 2004). The research in this book takes an experimental approach in areas where objectivity is required, for example Chapter Four Interactive Pedagogical Feedback.

It also employs the cyclical nature of action research to contribute with theory and practice as can be seen in the case of Chapter Five Interactive Audio Feedback.

3.3 Methods

It is relevant in this section to highlight the distinction between the methodology and methods of the investigation. Methodology focuses on the framework that structures the data-collecting process, and enables the implementation of theory while methods refer to tools for data collection.

A range of methods were used in the research performed for this book that draw on both empirical and opinion-based research methods. The fact that different research methods offer possible solutions for various problems, and represent important critical perspectives in the nature of the research (Brewer, & Hunter, 1989) makes the selection of the appropriate method(s) important.

There are three basic methods of collecting data. Post-test scores were taken to determine learner performance, and surveys and interviews were also used in this study.

The survey research method was utilized to grab learner and lecturer perceptions of interactivity in the required experiments.

Analysing qualitative data is a complicated matter owing to the variety of approaches followed by different researchers (Dey, 2003). Selecting the right approach depends upon the data and the specific purpose of the researcher. However, the rich variety of ideas makes the matter complicated. Tesch (1990) has identified three main orientations that encompass these multiple perspectives. The former allows the researcher to identify any "language-orientated" approaches. This perspective focuses on the language and how people communicate, and comprehend their interactions. In the second orientation, the researchers identify any "descriptive-interpretive" approaches that provide description and interpretation of the social phenomena. The latter orientation identifies "theory-building" approaches that are orientated to find connections between social phenomena. Qualitative data obtained from interviews are analysed to categorise the information following different procedures.

Dey (2003), for example, describe a series of steps from the first encounter to the data until the categories have been created that include finding a focus, managing the data, reading and annotating, categorizing and linking the data connecting the categories, corroborating evidences producing an account, creating and assigning the categories, and splitting and splicing. This process, generally named coding by researchers (Maxwell & Miller, 2008), is used in this book to analyse the interviews. The procedure involves segmenting and labelling the data into discrete units. These units are grouped into categories that are compared among each other. The coding process creates a similarity-based ordering of data that replaces the original contiguity-based ordering. However, critics (Tesch, 1990) referred to this replacement of an original connected structure by a different, categorical structure as "decontextualizing and re-contextualizing". They perceive that the lack of the original context in this procedure of coding and other categorizing strategies as a major defect.

The methods in Chapter 5 are triangulated on the search for validity and reliability. The scores obtained in different experiment for example are evaluated and compared against the opinion of the students and lecturers obtained after experiments are finished.

Triangulation encompasses observation and evaluation of several angles of the problem under study. Triangulation in general terms is defined as "the combination of methodologies in the study of the same phenomenon" (Jick, 1979). In the social sciences, triangulation seeks to validate the research process by using more than one method. The concurrence between the methods labelled by Denzin (1978) as "between (or across) methods" reinforces the results and increase validation.

For example, determination of the speed enhancement in Chapter Five Interactive Audio Feedback was studied by interviewing the lecturers, observing their behaviour, and evaluating performance. Although the focus was always on the speed enhancement of the audio feedback, data collection has been diversified. The use of multiple and independent measures arriving at the same conclusions depicts a more certain image of the phenomenon.

The following three chapters describe the experiments developed to test the effects of interactivity in the context of the educational triangle.

CHAPTER FOUR

INTERACTIVE PEDAGOGICAL FEEDBACK

4.1 Introduction

This research aims to introduce evidence on how pedagogically-designed formative feedback enhances e-learning environments through the practical implementation of ISAQ within an e-learning environment (Palacios and Evans, 2010).

It considers the impact that different levels of interactivity have on students' memory and understanding. In particular, it considers the use of pedagogical feedback in the form of interactive self-assessment questions (ISAQ) as a mechanism to promoting learning when using an e-learning system. A general feature of the two e-learning system prototypes developed is the use of ISAQ to allow students to evaluate their grasp of the material with a view to revisiting it if they feel it to be necessary.

Two experiments were developed to complement each other and to determine if any contrasts can be made between them. Following the action research methodologies, any pitfalls detected and lesson learned in the initial experiment were taken into account in the second experiment and subsequent activities. Both case studies consider whether the incorporation of ISAQ has a measurable impact on learning, as indicated by their performance in applied tests. It is believed that the addition of feedback will significantly enhance the learning experience because it will contribute to the development of higher order cognitive skills.

The ISAQ seem to improve the capacity of the memories described in the cognitive model of learning (Sweller, 1988) by relating previous knowledge stored in LTM to new information being processed in more limited and less permanent memories (see page **23**) which is consistent with the theory of generative learning (see page **24**). STM and WM hold much less information than LTM, which is considered to be a huge reservoir for data accumulation. Information to be transferred from STM to WM and then to a more permanent location (LTM) requires the student to have the ability to extend what has been learned in one context to new contexts (Byrnes, 1996). Transfer is different to remembering facts or procedures as it carries more complexity in learning. The distinction between the two is of great value because the effectiveness of a learning system is enhanced when a higher learning activity such as transfer is achieved (Bransford et al., 2000).

The experiments and systems developed in both case studies are underpinned by the dual coding theory (Paivio, 1986), the cognitive load theory (Chandler & Sweller, 1991), the cognitive theory of multimedia learning (Mayer & Moreno, 1998b), and a constructivist learning approach (see **section 2.3** and **section 2.4**).

Authorware and a web-based multimedia e-learning system were used to create and deliver the lessons. They are ideal tools to complement or replace traditional delivery. e-Learning can be defined as a combination of technology and the pedagogical approaches that are required when presenting and teaching a particular subject. e-Learning systems are key delivery components to communicate the educational message by using text and visual images. The content was designed according to Mayer's (2001) multimedia principles of learning (see section 2.6.3).

Interactivity and the interaction model (see 2.6.2) have been studied in similar contexts before, but without considering the pedagogical benefits of ISAQ.

Assessment has been used in these experiments as part of the feedback mechanism (see page 43). Although assessment is generally considered to be a term that describes the process by which students are given tests and assigned grades, it is specifically a mechanism for providing either the teachers (summative assessment) or the learners (formative assessment) with vital information for improving their teaching/learning methodology and, if accompanied by feedback, to determine where mistakes have been made to reflect on them and to become more effective, self-assessing, self-directed learners (Angelo & Cross, 1993).

However, for the technology to work effectively it must embrace pedagogical methods to elicit performance and provide a well guided element of interactivity. For ISAQ to be effective, they must be designed following well established design principles (Mayer, 2001). When these principles are applied to the design of web learning content, it creates a playground in which deep learning can be fostered and where interactivity plays a crucial role in student education (Evans & Sabry, 2002). A basic characteristic of interactivity is learner control of the pace of a multimedia presentation; this is useful as students learn better when they are allowed to control the pace of presentation of a narrated animation (Mayer & Chandler, 2001). Research studies that allow students the freedom to interact and keep control of their own pace while learning in a computer-based simulation have shown evidence of higher performance (Mayer et al., 2003). Research on the effect of interactivity indicates that learner performance increases when they are exposed to a system that interactively reacts to their using ISAQ (Evans & Gibbons, 2007). In the two experiments investigated, both consider the effect of adding ISAQ to a computer-based system already used by undergraduate students. Evans & Gibbons (2007) describe ISAQ as computer-based multiple-choice or text-entry questions that require input from the learner, and provide feedback based on that input. Each case involved two different types of ISAQ, designed to engage either memory (retention) or understanding (transfer) in an effort to determine which is the most effective. The studies look at retention and transfer, as considered by Mayer (2001), where retention is the power to recognise or recall past learning events (surface learning), while the transfer skill involves recognition but also interpretation and implementation of that knowledge in a different context (deep learning).

For each experiment, a computer-based system was designed to teach a lesson about how the circulatory system and the heart work, similar to other experiments developed by Evans & Gibbons (2007) and Mayer (2001; 2003) on how a bicycle pump works. A non-interactive component was added as a control group for comparison reasons. The experiment looks to measure the (retention and transfer) learning effects taking place in the learners and provides a degree of the impact by measuring their scores. The hypothesis is that adding interactivity in the form of retention and transfer self-assessment questions to a computer-based system will increase learning. The prediction is made on the basis that ISAQ help the learner to identify misconceptions, create mental schemata that can be added to existing knowledge by providing constructive feedback, and integrate those schemata to form new skills or attitudes.

4.2 Experiment 1 (using Authorware)

4.2.1 Methodology

4.2.1.1 Participants

A group of 30 students aged between 21-30, from different ethnic backgrounds and of different genders. Recruitment was made via email notification on a first-come-first-served basis with a £5.00 reward for participating in the experiment. Participants were not informed of either the topic or the mechanism for knowledge acquisition. Students were randomly divided into three groups: 10 in the ISAQ group (with retention type interactive self-assessment questions), 10 in the ISAQ group (with transfer type interactive self-assessment questions), and 10 in the nISAQ group (non-interactive self-assessment questions). They share similar educational backgrounds and are all registered on MSc courses at Brunel University.

4.2.1.2 Materials and apparatus

Three interactive e-learning systems developed in Adobe Authorware 7 were designed to teach students how the heart and the circulatory system work. Their structure contains: a pre-test to determine the student's previous knowledge; the lesson explaining the heart's main parts, the circulatory system function and how both relate to the process of pumping blood around the body; and a post-test to assess what the student learned. A computer laboratory with thirty computers running Microsoft Windows XP was the environment used to implement the study. The three content-identical systems consisted of two containing ISAQ components (retention and transfers interactive self-assessment questions), and one without them (the nISAQ-non-interactive self-assessment question). After a brief **introduction** giving instructions on the procedures used to operate the simulation, personal information was collected to keep general statistics about the groups. Materials and apparatus were consistent with previous experiments developed by Evans (2008).

The pre-test consisted of four questions designed to determine the students' prior knowledge of the heart and the circulatory system. Two Likert-scale type questions were asked for each topic and presented to the learners before starting the lesson, where the learner was required to rate his/her knowledge from very low (1) to very high (see Figure 6). Another two open-ended questions were given asking the students to type in an explanation of how the heart and the circulatory system work (Figure 7).They allowed the learners to describe their previous knowledge of the subject.

The lesson consisted of two components: one related to the circulatory system and another to the heart. They kept this order during the online presentation. The lesson on the circulatory system focused on the 16 stages taken by the heart to pump the blood around the body (Figure 8 and Figure 9).

The lessons are presented in very interactive flash animation embedded in Authorware describing the stages below performed by the heart to pump blood around the body.

Atria systole
The left and right atrial muscles contract
The left and right atria decrease in volume
The pressure in the atria increases
The mitral and tricuspid valve open
Ventricular systole
The left and right ventricle muscles contract
The left and right ventricles decrease in volume
The pressure in v increases
The m and t valves close (muscle)
The semi lunar valves open
Blood flows into pulmonary artery and aorta
Atria and Ventricular diastole
Both muscles relax
Atria increases in volume
Pressure in v decreases
Semi lunar valves close
Blood flows into atria.

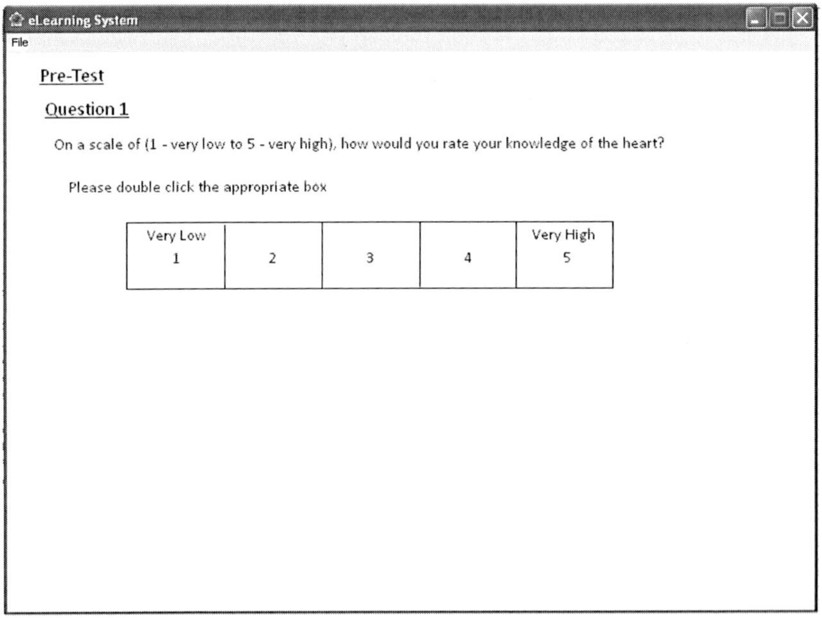

Figure 6: The Likert-scale pre-test question for each topic

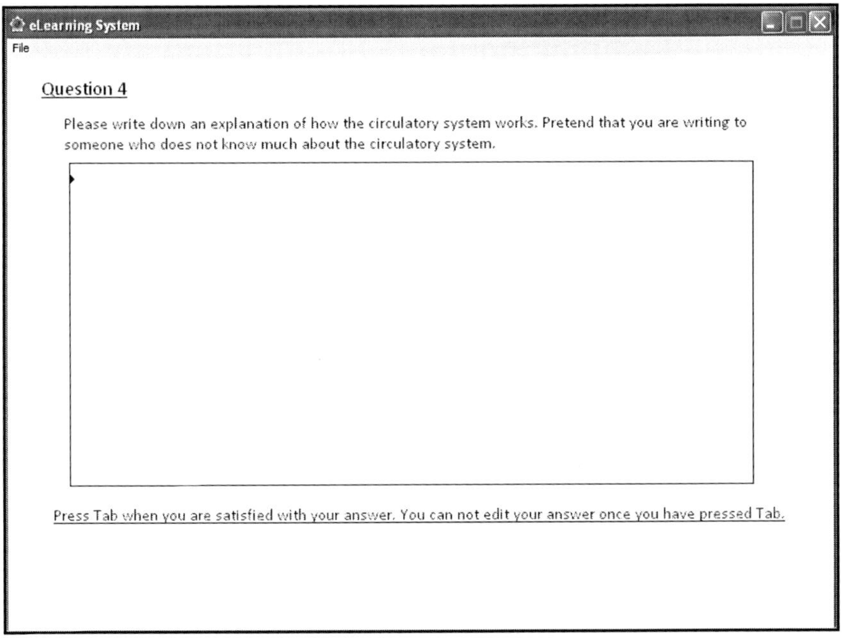

Figure 7: The open-ended type pre-test question

As can be seen in the previous list, these stages are related to the four cardiac cycles in the heart: the Atria and Ventricular systole (contraction) and the Atria and Ventricular diastole (dilatation). This corresponds to other studies performed by Evans's (2007) twelve-stage operation and Mayer and Gallini's (1990) ten-stage description, where the operation of a bicycle pump is used to study the effect of interactivity.

The ISAQ mechanism located after the lesson content and before the post-test consisted of eight multiple-choice questions. The pedagogical design used to build them offers constructive feedback for both correct and incorrect answers. The structure of the questions offers distracters, which are the incorrect answers presented as a choice in a multiple-choice test. The selected item could be dragged and dropped into an answer box (Figure 10).

Then, constructive feedback pops up with a related explanation; if incorrect, the learner is allowed to repeat the question. The learner controls the pace by means of two buttons located at the lower right part of the page; these are identical throughout the entire system.

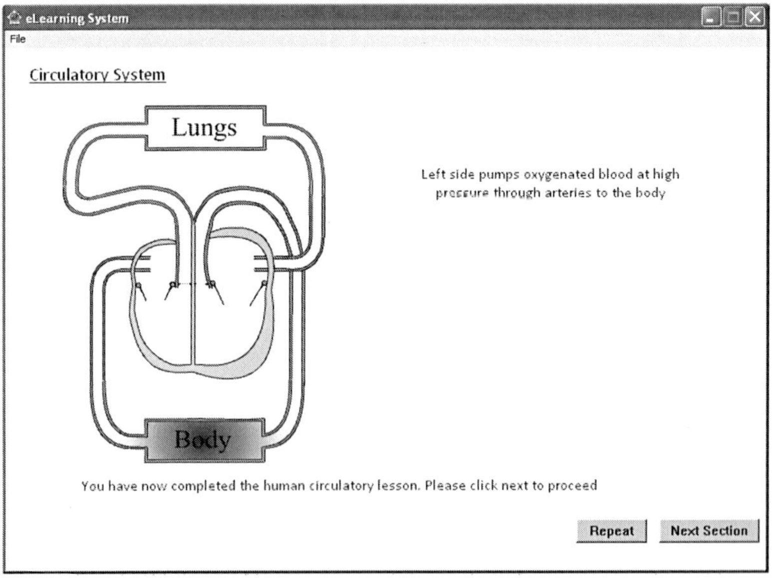

Figure 8: Screenshot of the animation representing the circulatory system.

The ISAQ questions for the transfer and retention systems differ from one another for obvious reasons. The retention ISAQ provide questions pedagogically designed for retention, while the transfer ISAQ provides questions for deep learning. They both differ from the nISAQ system, as that does not include any feedback at all. Both types of ISAQ were consistent with the lesson content. In other words, the ISAQ information was a formative assessment of the lesson material.

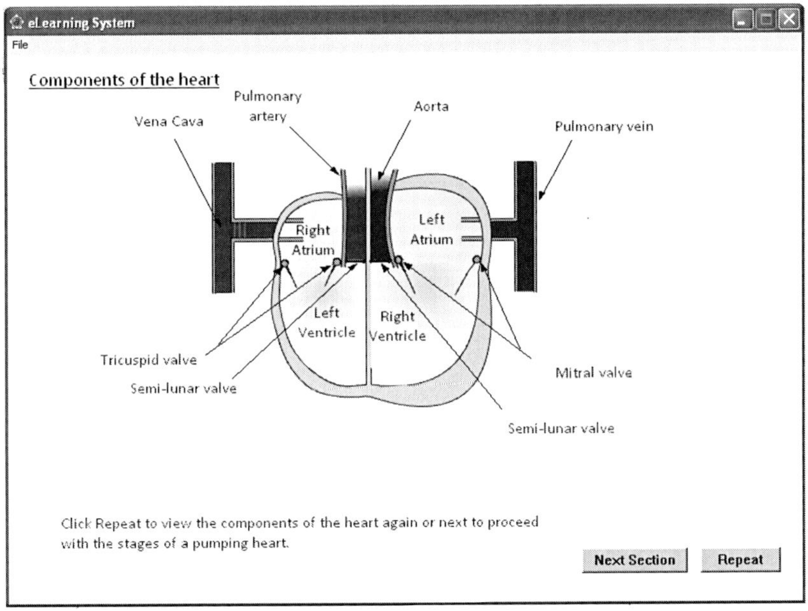

Figure 9: Screenshot of the animation describing parts of the heart

The next image (Figure 10) shows the initial interactive self-assessment question for the ISAQ systems. Dragging the right answer into the box triggers the feedback mechanism that allows the user to proceed to the next question.

The post-test (Figure 11) consisted of a summative assessment to determine the final score of the student. It measured how much the learner had retained or understood the lesson. It is located in the final part of the three systems and consisted of five retention questions and three transfer questions.

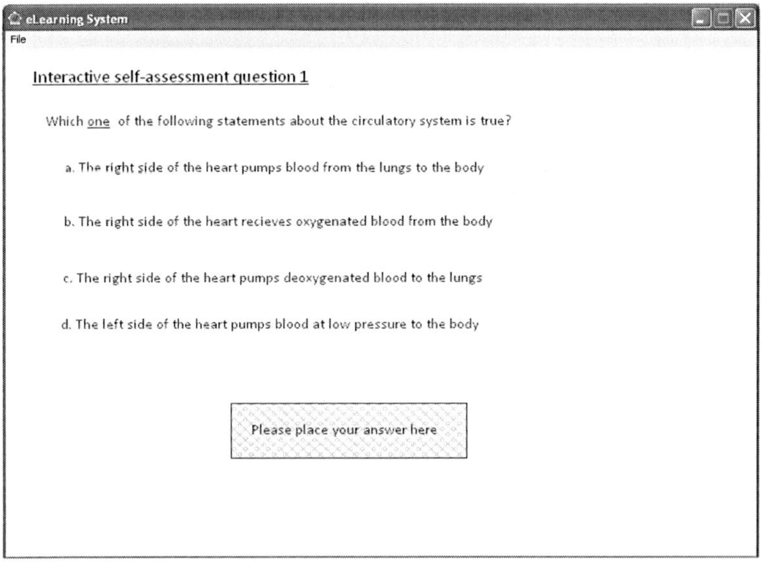

Figure 10: Interactive self-assessment question example.

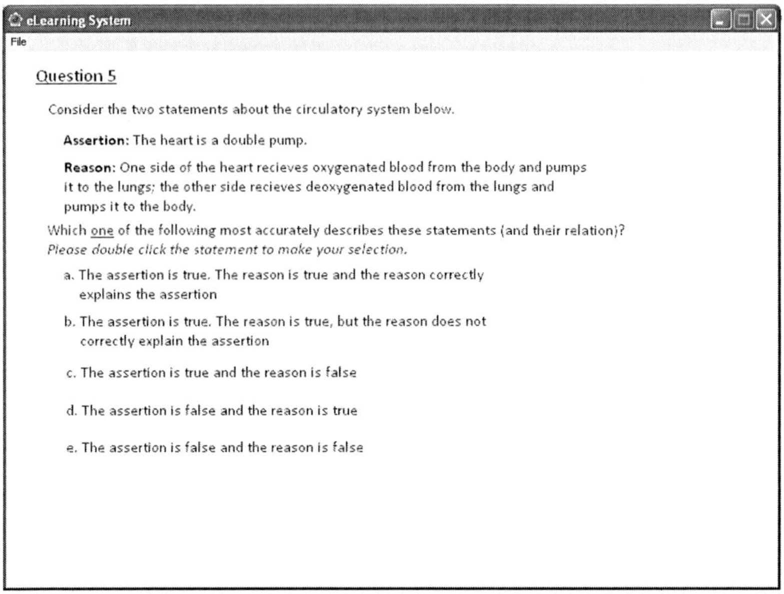

Figure 11: Example of a Post-test question

4.2.2 Results

The pre-test indicates that all three groups had low prior knowledge. It shows that all three groups possessed general prior knowledge about the heart function, as can be seen from a mean score of 45 per cent (SD=0.759). The majority (85 per cent) of students rated their knowledge of the "heart" higher than their knowledge of the "circulatory system". They rated their knowledge of the heart as (3) and of the circulatory system as (2) "little knowledge" in the Likert scale. The mean score average was 1.80 (SD.786) from a total of 25 possible marks.

	Post test scores for			
System n=10	**Retention questions**		**Transfer questions**	
	M (OUT OF 5)	SD	M (OUT OF 3)	SD
rISAQ	1.87	.98	.37	.51
tISAQ	1.68	1.27	.32	.49
nISAQ	1.32	.57	.25	.42

Table 2: Post-test scores (n) =10 for each group M=mean SD=Standard deviation

For the post-test, the means and standard deviations for the retention, transfer and control condition are given in **Table 2.**

The evidence suggests that students in the rISAQ (retention) system had the best (M=1.87) performance when compared to the tISAQ (transfer) system (M=1.68) and the nISAQ (control –No ISAQ) system (M=1.32) in terms of overall scores.

A one-way analysis of variance (ANOVA) was conducted. As can be seen the retention score is *F (.813) p=.454*. For an alpha level of .05 the power of the test is .46 (low). The size of the effect (Cohen's d) is 0.69 (medium).

The findings conclude that the use of ISAQ definitely enhances the learning experience. These results are consistent with the interactivity principle, which suggests that interactive self-assessment should increase learning by actively engaging students in the learning process.

A set of interviews were designed in order to collect the students' feedback. It was deduced from the interviews that participants were positive about the help obtained from the navigation mechanism used to control the pace and interaction in the systems. This is consistent with

Mayer & Anderson's (1992) experiments that found a negative effect for the absence of pacing control on test scores, leading to cognitive overload.

Students complained about the lesson structure and the clarity of the lesson, but rated the overall experience as positive. All students interviewed indicated that the overall experience exceeded their expectations. They also felt they had learned using the systems.

4.3 Experiment 2 (using Forceten)

4.3.1 Methodology

4.3.1.1 Participants

The participants are a group of 25 students aged between 18 and 30 years old from different ethnic backgrounds. The gender of the population is balanced, with 52 per cent female and 48 per cent male. Recruitment was performed in a Management of Information with Technology course. Participants were not informed about the subject of the topic or the mechanism for knowledge acquisition. Students were randomly divided into three groups: 8 in the ISAQ group (with retention type interactive self-assessment questions), 9 in the ISAQ group (with transfer type interactive self-assessment questions), and 8 in the nISAQ group (non-interactive self-assessment questions). They share similar educational backgrounds and are registered at Brunel University.

4.3.1.2 Materials and apparatus

Three interactive e-learning systems were designed to teach students how the heart and the circulatory system work. The interactive e-learning systems were constructed, and delivered using a browser-based proprietary Learning Content Management System (LCMS) called ForceTen. The technology employed in this virtual learning environment is object technology, as shown in Figure 4. Materials and apparatus are consistent with previous experiments developed by Evans (Evans, 2008), as indicated in experiment one.

Their structure contains a pre-test to determine students' previous knowledge; the lesson explaining the heart main parts, the circulatory system function and how these relate to the process of pumping the blood in the human body; and a post-test to assess what the student learned. A computer laboratory with thirty computers running Microsoft Windows XP was the environment used to implement the study. The three content-identical systems consisted of two containing ISAQ components (retention and transfer interactive self-assessment questions), and one without (the nISAQ—non-interactive self-assessment question).

The pre-test consisted of four questions. The two initial questions were designed to collect demographic information. Then the next question is composed of two Likert scale-type questions created to rate the student's knowledge from very low (1) to very high (5) of the heart and the circulatory system. The final two questions were open-ended, asking the user to type in an explanation of how the heart and the circulatory system work in order to check their prior knowledge (see Figure 12). This allowed the learners to describe their previous knowledge of the subject. Marking was performed on all 4 questions in base 4.

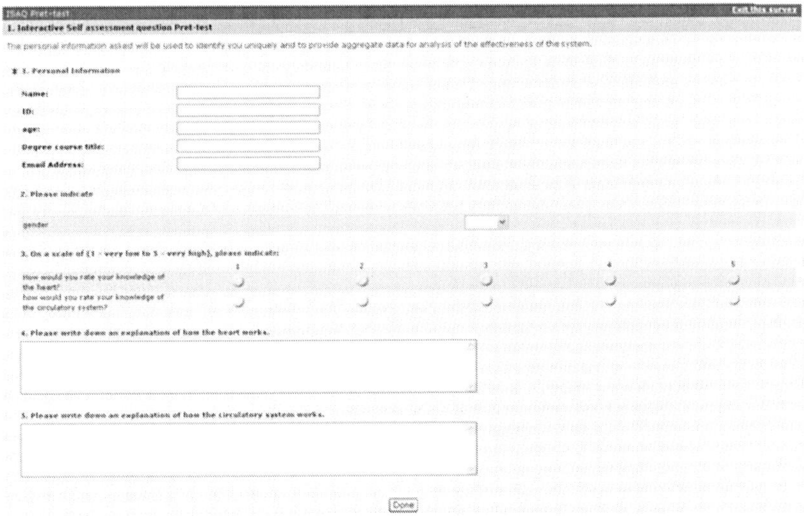

Figure 12: Experiment 2 pre-test questions.

The lesson consisted of two components: one related to the circulatory system and another to the heart. They kept this order during the online presentation. The section on the circulatory system focused on the 16 stages taken by the heart to pump the blood around the body (See Figure 13). The second element of the lesson described the whole cycle followed by the heart to pump the blood around the body (See Figure 14).

The ISAQ mechanism located after the lesson content and before the post-test consisted of 4 multiple choice questions.

Figure 15 is a screenshot showing a transfer ISAQ system. The Screenshot shows that dragging the right answer into the box triggers the feedback mechanism that allows the user to proceed.

Figure 16 is a screenshot of the retention ISAQ.

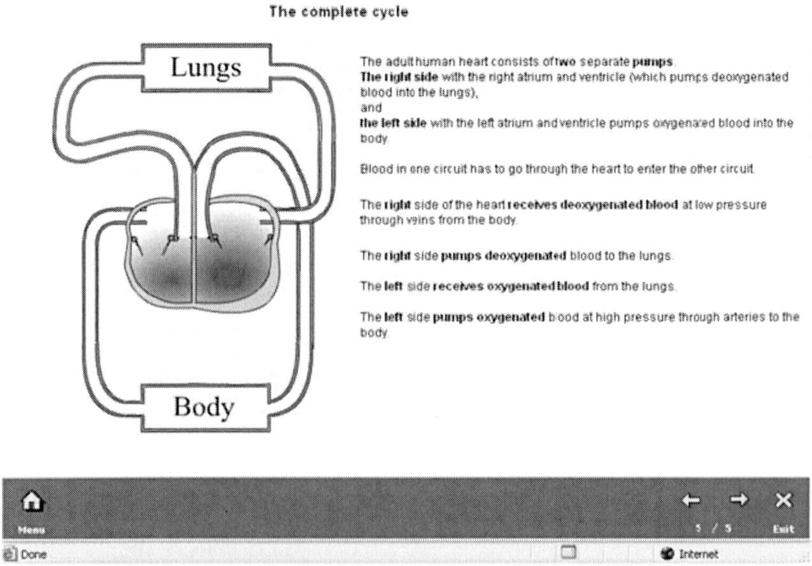

Figure 13: Screenshot of the animation with main functions in the circulatory systems.

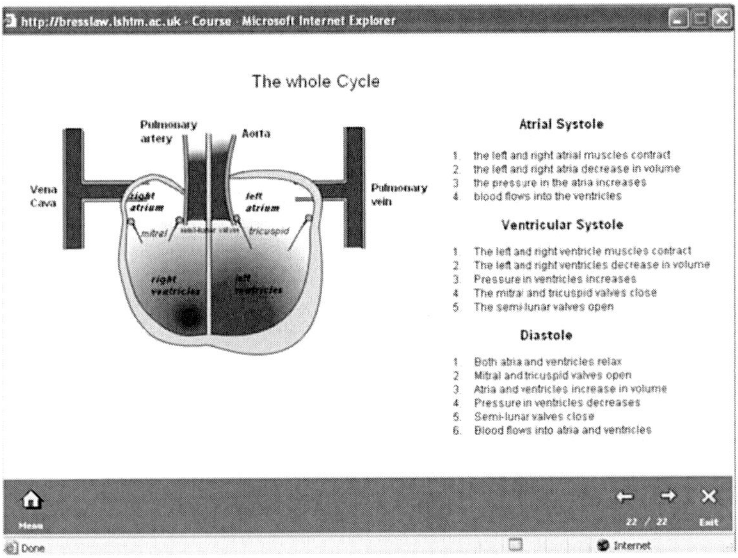

Figure 14: Screenshot of the animation describing the whole cycle in the heart

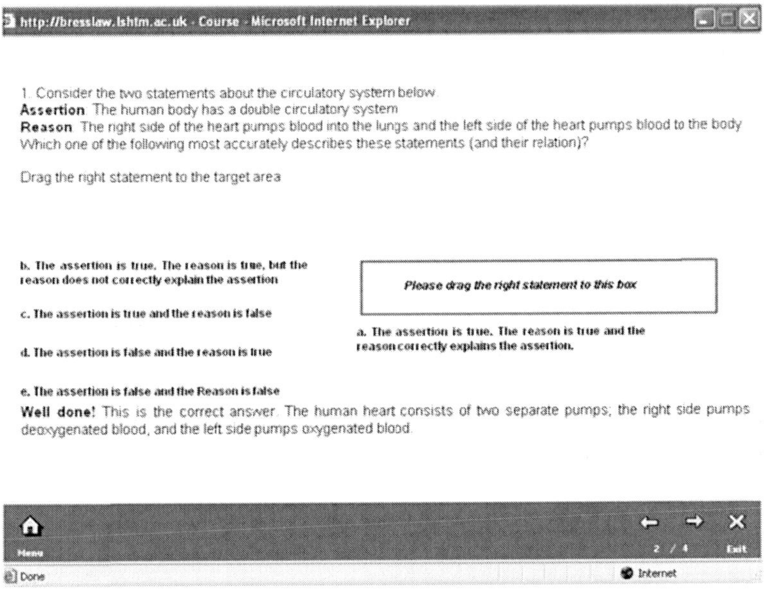

Figure 15: The Screenshot shows an ISAQ for the transfer system.

The pedagogical design used to build the ISAQ considers constructive feedback for both correct and incorrect answers. The structure of the questions uses distracters, which are incorrect answers presented as a choice in a multiple-choice test. The selected item could be dragged and dropped into an answer box, then constructive feedback would pop up with an explanation; if incorrect, the learner is allowed to repeat the question.

The post-test (see Figure 17 and 18) consisted of a summative assessment that determined the final score of the student. It measured how much the learner retained or understood about the lesson. It is located in the final part of all the three systems and consisted of five retention questions and three transfer questions.

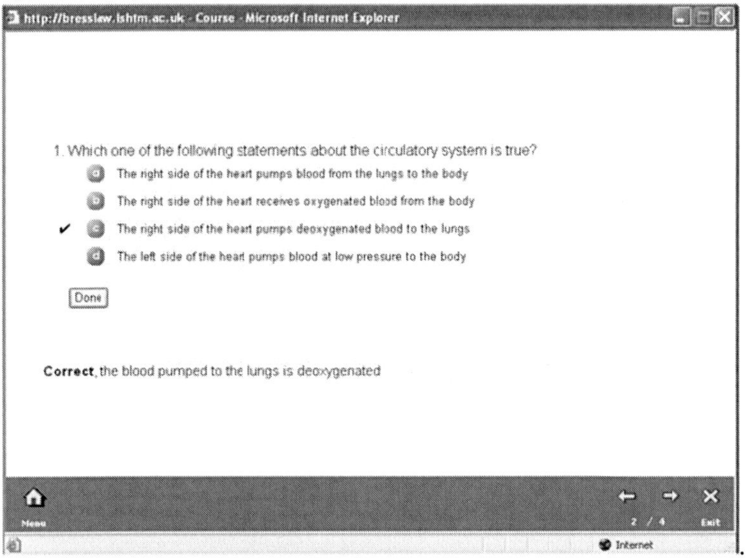

Figure 16: Screenshot showing an ISAQ for the retention system.

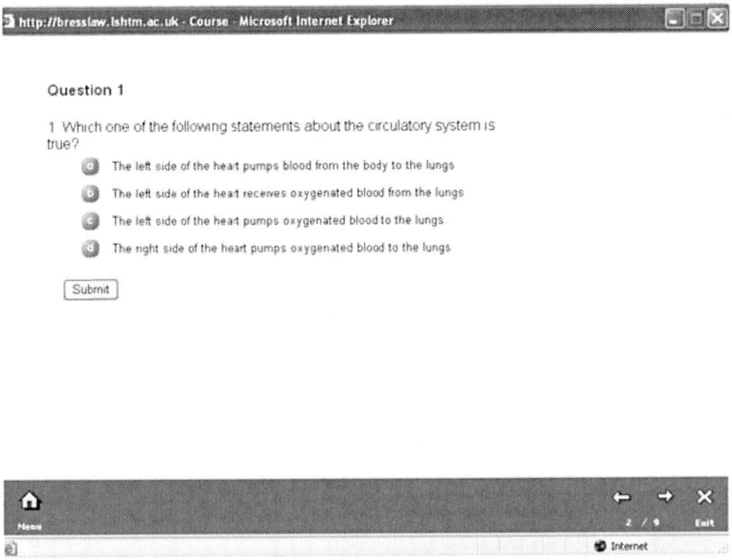

Figure 17: Screenshot showing questions to measure retention in the post-test.

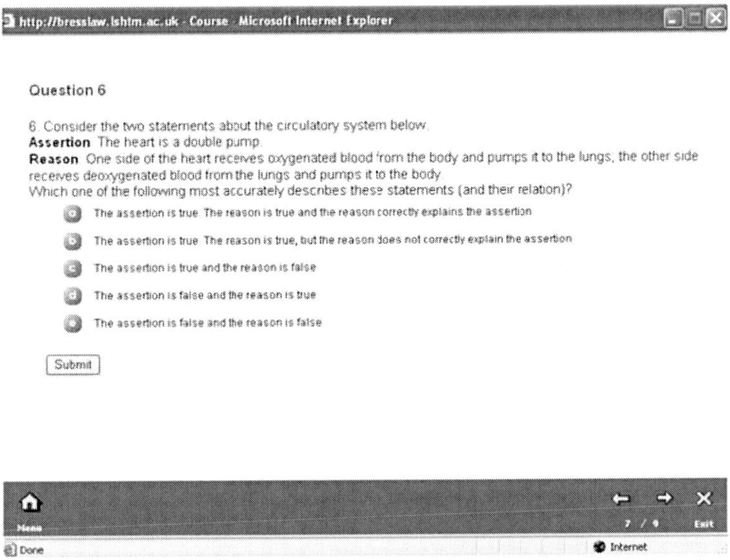

Figure 18: Screenshot showing a question to measure transfer in the post-test.

4.3.2 Results

The pre-test indicates that all three groups had low prior knowledge. It revealed that all three groups believed their knowledge of the heart to be greater than the post-test revealed. The circulatory questions had a mean of 2.64 (sd=0.907); and the circulatory system a mean of 2.40 (sd=0.957).

The best post-test score within the three systems was 3.1 (sd=0.59) out of a maximum score of 4 for the transfer questions. The mean and standard deviations for the retention and transfer tests are given in Table 1. For an alpha level of .05 the power of the test is .93 (>.8, reasonable). The size of the effect (Cohen's d) is 1.48 (large).

System Type	Post test scores for Retention questions		Transfer questions	
	M (OUT OF 5)	SD	M(OUT OF 3)	SD
rISAQ n=8	2.6	.44	1.33	1
tISAQ n=9	3.1*	.59	1.88	.38
nISAQ n=8	1.7	1.20	0.88	.44

Table 3: Post-test scores * p < .05, M=mean SD=Standard deviation

There is significant difference in the t test scores, $F(2,22) = 6.86$, $p < .05$. A one-way ANOVA with a Turkey HSD post hoc test for all pairwise comparisons reveals a significant difference between the tISAQ and nISAQ retention score.

4.4 Chapter Discussion

The object of this experiment was to determine to what extent, if any, learning is increased when using pedagogical feedback in the form of ISAQ within multimedia e-learning systems.

The existence of a learning effect and its two types (retention or transfer) were investigated. Retention relates to recall from memory and transfer is related to deep learning. The results definitely indicate that a learning effect has been detected in both experiments #1 and #2 that is consistent with the principle of interactivity. Statistically significant differences were found for retention tests in Experiment 1 and transfer tests in Experiment 2 (compared to the control group).

Furthermore, in Experiment 1 the results indicate that the two groups with ISAQ (retention and transfer conditions) got a better performance than the control group in terms of overall scores. When the two groups embedded with the ISAQ are compared, the group with the retention condition performed better than the group with the transfer condition. The experiment indicates that ISAQ actually increase memory.

In Experiment 2, the results show that the two groups with ISAQ (retention and transfer conditions) again got a better performance than the control group. But when the two groups embedded with the ISAQ are compared, the group with the transfer condition performs better than the group with the retention condition. These may be interpreted as an indication that the use of ISAQ promotes deep learning. Although the results at the level of the retention and transfer conditions seem to be contradictory, they may be explained by the differences in LCMS that were used to deliver the lesson (see 0).

The differences were tested using one-tailed independent sample Student's t-tests. These were chosen for their reliability even when sample sizes are small ($n<30$), and robustness in the presence of unequal variances in the populations being compared. The generizability is indicated by the probability of a Type I Error (incorrectly rejecting the null hypothesis) which is alpha=.05 or equivalently a confidence level of 95 per cent.

Post hoc calculations of required sample sizes are usually regarded as uninformative (Hoenig, J.M., Heisey, D.M. (2001). The abuse of power. The American Statistician, 55(1), 19–24). However, it is possible to estimate the probability of having correctly rejected the null hypothesis by calculating the power. For an alpha level of .05 the power of the test in experiment 1 is .46 (low) and for experiment 2 is .93 (>.8, reasonable). The size of the effect (Cohen's d) is 0.69 (medium) for experiment 1 and 1.48 (large) for experiment 2.

The reliability of statistical results is additionally indicated by the extent to which they can be reproduced. Experiment 2 was constructed in order to confirm the reliability of the results from experiment 1, which it did by indicating that the experimental groups outperformed the control group.

The effects of interactivity in this experiment are consistent with the generative theory of learning (Wittrock, 1974).

According to the theory, learning is the result of concrete associations generated by the learner between his or her prior experience and the present learning activity. The ISAQ seems to engage student attention and facilitate the transfer of information from STM to LTM. The process may be result of the inherent properties of interactivity that allows the learner to navigate through the content to grab the required information to form the mental scheme in the LTM area.

CHAPTER FIVE

INTERACTIVE AUDIO FEEDBACK

5.1 Introduction

The production of feedback on submitted work is widely regarded as an important formative part of learning in higher education institutions (Gikandi, et al, 2011). In the past, producing feedback has meant creating handwritten comments on students' scripts or on a separate sheet. Many tutors have progressed from handwritten to providing effective typewritten (word-processed) ones.

For most people, speaking is a much quicker form of communication than typing (Gould, 1982). People experimenting with writing and speaking letters under various conditions demonstrate that speaking required only 35-75 per cent of the time that writing did. The reason is perhaps founded on the fact that speaking as an innate part of human behaviour is more universal than writing, which was invented around 5000 years ago (Cleland, 2006).

In addition, the sounds produced when we speak include structures classified as paralinguistic, e.g. prosody and rhythm, and as linguistic, e.g. phonology, syntax (Shankar, 2006). The linguistics and syntactic structures can be easily transported to written expression. On the contrary, those paralinguistic structures based in music and rhythms are lost in translation.

The possibility for people with poor computer skills to interact with technology has now made it relatively easy to record and return audio feedback as an alternative to typewritten feedback. It will produce the immediate benefit of reducing the time to create the feedback and complement it with some paralinguistic structural components, which are not present in writing. The present research seeks to establish whether the use of such interactive technology can enhance the feedback process for both tutors and learners.

Whilst handwritten or typewritten feedback seems to be the norm, there is evidence to suggest that spoken feedback can be much more easily generated. Furthermore, developmental studies indicate that written skills develop much later than oral skills and take more cognitive processing to exercise (Grabowski, 2010). This cognitive overhead may partially explain why most people find it quicker to speak than to write. This suggests that one mechanism for reducing the heavy load for creating feedback might be to use the spoken rather than written modality.

Several studies have considered the relative speeds of speaking and writing. In early informal studies Gould (1978) suggested that people could handwrite memorized material at about 40 words per minute (wpm) but speak or read it aloud at around 200 wpm. Card et al. (1983) report that an experienced typist can reach approx. 80 wpm. Of course, the process of generating feedback is not simply a matter of speaking or writing. It also involves the critical evaluation of students' work and the synthesis of sentences. Audio feedback has the promise of being quicker than entering text into a word processor, and is often regarded as richer and more personalized by students.

The study involved determining whether the speed enhancements of speaking rather than typing are carried over to the process of creating feedback. The investigation therefore sought to test the hypothesis (H1) that suggests creating feedback in audio form is quicker than creating feedback in typewritten form.

The investigation also analysed whether the phonetic benefits of audio over typewritten feedback are carried over to the learner. The study thus also sought to test the hypothesis (H2) that feedback received in audio form is better quality than feedback received in written form.

In order to test these hypotheses, four experiments were designed. The first was a pilot study (5.2 Pilot Experiment (Experiment One)) to test the time-reduction hypothesis H1. On the basis of the pilot study outcome, two additional studies (0 5.3 Experiment Two and 5.5 Experiment Four) were designed to corroborate the time-reduction hypothesis H1 (under slightly different conditions). Students' opinions were collected (0 5.4 Experiment Three) to test the quality-enhancement hypothesis H2. All these experiments are described in the following paragraphs of this section.

Action research cycles (look at **MISSING**)—considered in this study as the methodological approach—contribute to the collection of feedback from lectures and students involved in all the experiments (0, 0, 0, 0) prior to, during, and after the implementation of the research activities, in order to envisage the right experiment design and determine the specific benefits of audio versus typewriting feedback as mentioned in the Literature review.

5.2 Pilot Experiment (Experiment One)

5.2.1 Method

5.2.1.1 Participants

The subject was a male Senior Lecturer in Emotional Labour at Brunel University in West London, UK, using assignment essays submitted by undergraduate students taking a BSc in Business and Management.

5.2.1.2 Materials and apparatus

Audio feedback (speech) was recorded using an Olympus WS-310M handheld digital voice recorder as a WMA file. Text feedback was recorded (typed) using Microsoft Word 2007, a Viglen PC and a 17" TFT display. It was stored as a Windows .docx file.

The following questionnaire was designed to capture the lecturer's opinion and identify the effectiveness of audio feedback in the final assignment. The questionnaire structure contains ten questions that focus on determining the lecturer's previous experience, expectations, possible outcomes and attitudes toward using audio feedback and/or written feedback.

AUDIO VERSUS TEXT FEEDBACK Lecturer questionnaire	
1.	Describe the main reason to consider audio versus text feedback.
2.	What were your expectations about the possible outcome?
3.	Do you feel the expected outcome was achieved and why?
4.	Did you expect any drawbacks, explain?
5.	Do you think, if any, the drawback(s) were as you expected?
6.	Do you think audio is more successful than text feedback?
7.	Were there any problem(s) that you didn't expect?
8.	Would you do anything different if you do it again?
9.	Would you use audio feedback for real in the future?
10.	Do you have any additional comment or suggestion?

5.2.1.3 Procedure

Two one-hour marking slots were assigned for conducting the experiment. The submitted assignments were randomly divided into two groups. The scripts had all been read on a previous occasion and handwritten notes had been made on the scripts, but no feedback had been formally recorded or created.

The first group of scripts was used for the audio feedback condition (A). During the first allotted hour, each script was re-read and audio feedback was recorded. Thinking and reading time formed part of the measure in an effort to capture as close as possible the real world conditions of a lecturer generating and recording feedback. The process was conducted for each script in the pile until one hour had elapsed. The number of complete feedback recordings was then noted. For the text feedback condition (T), the second batch of scripts was used. During the second allotted hour, as in the first, each script was re-read and feedback was recorded, this time in typed form. The number of complete feedback recordings was again noted. Subsequent to the feedback recording, the tutor was interviewed using the previous questionnaire.

5.2.2 Results

The number of scripts processed with audio feedback in the one-hour slot was eight, and the number of scripts processed with text feedback in one hour was four.

The completed Lecturer questionnaire is attached below.

AUDIO VERSUS TEXT FEEDBACK
Lecturer questionnaire

1. Describe the main reason to consider audio versus text feedback.
I feel more comfortable working with audio than with text feedback.
2. What were your expectations about the possible outcome?
Completely positive. …I think that will reduce and facilitate my job.
3. Do you feel the expected outcome was achieved, and why?
Yes…because I could produce more student feedbacks in a shorter amount of time.
4. Did you expect any drawbacks? Explain.
Yes…the transformation of the files to MP3 files and the whole process until they are inserted in the system ready for the student to hear it. It will be cumbersome.
5. Do you think the drawback(s), if any, were as you expected?
No…because the Dictaphone facilitated the recording task and he managed to upload all 8 MP3 files.
6. Do you think audio is more successful than text feedback?
Yes, because it helped me to save time.

7. Were there any problem(s) that you didn't expect?
After listening to the first he noticed quite a few "ums" and "ers" that he expects to avoid with more practice.
8. Would you do anything different if you did it again?
Not many things....the practice will help to improve the procedure and I feel that I can do it faster.
9. Would you use audio feedback for real in the future?
Yes, absolutely.
10. Do you have any additional comments or suggestions?

I must say that I felt very at ease giving audio feedback. It felt very unconstrained, like free-wheeling down a hill with plenty of elbow room either side. After an hour I did not experience any flagging of energy and certainly no sudden sag in enthusiasm, which I admit to getting when marking conventionally...

5.2.3 Discussion

The experiment suggests that audio feedback doubles the number of scripts that can be processed in an hour (and, equivalently, reduces the time taken to process text feedback by 50 per cent). The lecturer's comments emphasised the usefulness of recording feedback as indicated in the questionnaire. This provides initial support for the time-reduction hypothesis H_1.

When interviewed, the tutor in this pilot experiment reported that he felt more comfortable working with audio than text feedback. He particularly appreciated the increase in the recording rate facilitated by audio. He reported that he had erroneously expected the creation and uploading of MP3 files to be much more complex than it turned out to be. The only reported drawback was the number of "ums" and "ers" that were recorded; but he expected this to decrease with practice. He added, "It felt very unconstrained, like free-wheeling down a hill with plenty of elbow room either side. After an hour I did not experience any flagging of energy and certainly no sudden sag in enthusiasm, which I admit to getting when marking conventionally".

In order to subject the findings to statistical analysis, the experiment was repeated, this time recording the time taken for each script so that a mean could be established and subjected to significance testing.

5.3 Experiment Two

5.3.1 Method

5.3.1.1 Participants

The subject was a male Senior Lecturer in Marketing at Brunel University in West London, UK, using dissertation proposals submitted by eight postgraduate students taking an MSc in Marketing. The tutor's mean typing speed was 24 words per minute, assessed using the average of two tests.

5.3.1.2 Materials and apparatus

Audio feedback (speech) was recorded using an Olympus WS-310M handheld digital voice recorder as a WMA file. Text feedback was recorded (typed) using Microsoft Word 2007, a Viglen PC and a 17" TFT display. It was stored as a Windows .docx file. Typing speed was assessed using Mavis Beacon Teaches Typing™.

5.3.1.3 Procedure

A random sample of eight MSc dissertation proposals was divided into two groups. The scripts had all been read on a previous occasion but no feedback had been recorded.

The first group of four scripts was used for the text feedback condition (T). For each script, the start time was recorded at the point where typing began, and the end time at the point where typing was completed to the satisfaction of the tutor. The reading time prior to commencement of typing did not form part of the measure. However, reading time during the construction of feedback was included.

For the audio feedback condition (A), again the start time was recorded at the point the recorder was first switched on, and the end time at the point where recording was completed to the satisfaction of the tutor. The tutor was permitted to pause the recording at any time to re-read the script or collect his thoughts. This thinking/reading time was included in the overall time. Significant differences between the times were assessed using a one-tailed Student's t-test. All statistical tests were performed with an alpha (α) value (significance threshold) of .05. Subsequent to the feedback recording, the tutor and A condition students were interviewed.

5.3.2 Results

In Experiment Two, the average time taken to produce the text feedback was 8:26.5 min and to produce the audio feedback was 5:07.5 min (see Table 4). Thus the use of audio reduced the overall feedback time by 39 per cent. The mean difference of -199 s (3:19 min) is statistically reliable, unpaired Student's *t*-test, $t(6) = -2.854$, one-tailed, $p < .05$, with an effect size of 2.02 (small).

Group	**Recording Time/s**	
	M	*SD*
T (n-4)	506.50	99.07
A (n=4)	307.50*	98.12

**p < .05; ES = 2.02*

Table 4: Experiment 2 Feedback Recording Times (in seconds)

5.3.3 Discussion

This study (Experiment Two) confirms the time-reduction hypothesis H_1 that audio recording can decrease the time it takes to create feedback by 39 per cent.

The tutor reported that he expected audio feedback to be beneficial because he believed students preferred it, and he thought it would be a "richer" medium. However the experience led him to think that there was actually no significant time saving (contrary to the reality; the findings were obviously unknown to him at the time). He also reported that in trying to balance the quality in the two modes he believed that the audio did not end up being richer. Despite these reservations he preferred recording audio feedback because the spoken word "is more natural" and "a lot of [wasted] effort is spent in typing the letters".

The students' perceptions did not match those of the tutor. They praised the audio feedback for feeling "extremely personal" and "less abstract than written text".

The students also suggested that audio "helped the relationship by reinforcing the professional bond between tutor and tutee". One interviewee commented that because he could "hear rustling paper, he knew the tutor had taken time to read through it".

Interviewees also commented that tonal feedback on "how good it is or not" made him feel the "information was richer" than written text. Another commented, "I prefer audio because you get the additional layers of feedback in the form of tonal suggestion". One added, "if it is more time-efficient than written feedback it is definitely worth it because it is a richer standard of feedback".

One related new effect that emerged from interviews was authenticity. One interviewee suggested that audio feedback was "more reliable because you can hear them flicking through your essay in the background", and "more rewarding and enjoyable because the tutor is perceived to have put in the effort". Another commented that the audio "reinforced that they had actually read through it". These learner effects all support the quality-enhancement hypothesis H_2.

5.4 Experiment Three

Following the initial successful experiments providing audio feedback for replacing text feedback, a follow up study to support the hypothesis H2 regarding quality enhancement was developed for the MBA course. Audio as summative feedback was provided to inform on students' final assessment.

5.4.1 Method

5.4.1.1 Participants

The subject was a male Senior Lecturer in Emotional Labour at Brunel University in West London, UK, using final assignment essays submitted by postgraduate students taking the module "Managing for the future" for their Master in Business and Administration.

5.4.1.2 Materials and apparatus

Audio feedback (speech) was recorded as an mp3 file using Audacity audio software installed on a Viglen PC using windows XP. Audacity® is open source software for recording and editing sounds.

Text feedback was recorded (typed) using Microsoft Word 2007, a Viglen PC and a 17" TFT display. It was stored as a Windows .docx file.

In addition, a questionnaire (Figure 19) was designed to capture the opinion of the students and identify the effectiveness of audio feedback in the final assignment.

The questionnaire structure encompasses three main areas. An initial area that requires demographic information such as date of birth, native language, age, gender and country of origin for example: Date, Module, Native Language, Age, Gender, Country of Origin.

A second area in the questionnaire focuses on previous experience, devices used and the technical difficulties faced and initial attitude before or at the moment the students have received the feedback. e.g.

5. Which form of feedback would you prefer (tick one only)?
Audio ____
Written ____

Then, a final area that evaluates student opinion after feedback has been received. A Likert scale is introduced in these question areas to evaluate accessibility of the feedback, if it is considered a valuable contribution, a contribution to learning, and the students' expectations about use of audio feedback in other courses, or coursework for example.

"I found the use of audio feedback contributed to my learning"
a. Strongly Disagree ____
b. Disagree ____
c. Neutral ____
d. Agree ____
e. Strongly agree ____

It was designed to determine the experience and the tools employed for listening to the feedback. The questionnaire also investigates accessibility to the audio file, how valuable the students consider the audio feedback, contribution to the students learning, and interest in using the audio feedback in the future in other courses.

MB5526 Managing for the Future
Audio Feedback for final assignment Survey

Luis Palacios (cbpglpp@brunel.ac.uk)

The purpose of this survey is to identify the effectiveness of Audio feedback in the final assignment

Date:		Native Language	
Module		Gender	
Age		Country of origin	

1. Have you experienced audio or video feedback in the past?
   Audio ____
   Video ____
   Both ____
   No ____

2. What device you use to listen your audio feedback?
   a. i-phone ____
   b. Brunel computer ____
   c. PC computer ____
   d. Mac computer ____
   e. Laptop ____
   f. Blackberry ____
   h. other (____________) ____

3. How long after you received the audio feedback file did you wait before listening to it?
   a. immediately ____
   b. same day ____
   c. Next day ____
   d. 2 to 7 day ____
   e. after a week ____

4. Did you face any technical problems listening to the file? Yes____ No____
If yes, please specify____

5. Which form of feedback would you prefer (tick one only)?
   Audio _
   Written ____

	Strongly disagree	Disagree	Neutral	Agree	Strongly agree
6. "I found the use of audio feedback accessible"					
7. "I found the use of audio feedback a valuable contribution					
8. "I would like to see continued use of audio feedback for my coursework"					
9. "I found the use of audio feedback contributed to my learning "					
10. "I would like to see audio feedback used for other courses at Brunel"					

Figure 19: Experiment 3- Questionnaire to capture student opinion

5.4.2 Procedure

Audio feedback was produced following the same procedure as indicated in the experiment one. Then, it was delivered to a group of regular MBA students as interactive feedback for their final assignments by dropping the audio feedback file and the questionnaire into the student's u-Link account (u-Link is the Blackboard learning content management system personalised for Brunel University). The audio file feedback is in MP3 format. The students listen to the audio file, complete the questionnaire and send it back by dropping the completed questionnaire in the lecturer's u-Link account.

5.4.3 Results

The results from the students' surveys are described as follows.

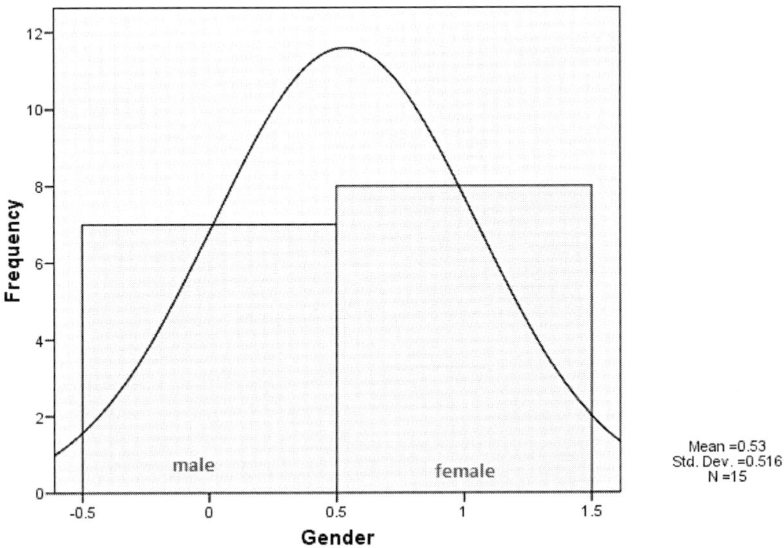

Figure 20: Gender distribution

The sample (N = 15) of postgraduate students was composed of 7 (46.7 per cent) males and 8 (53.3 per cent) females.

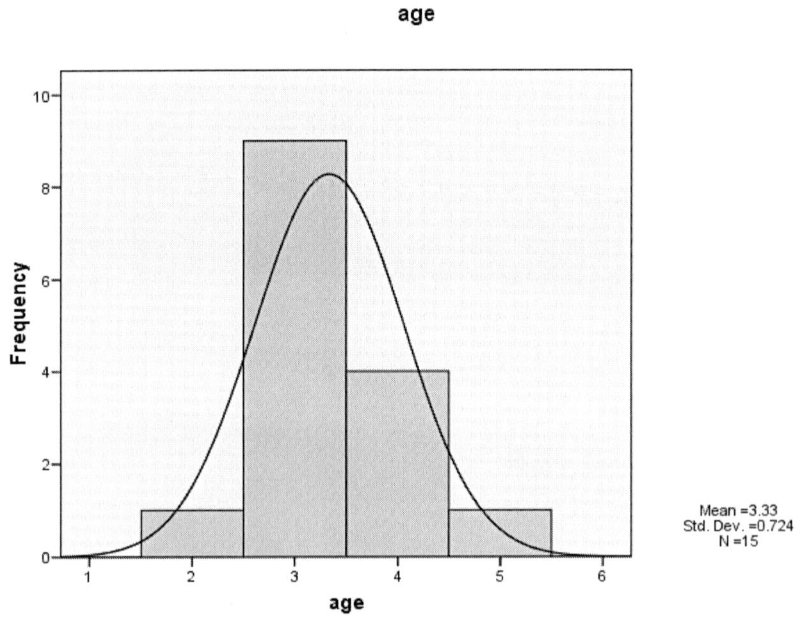

Figure 21: Age distribution

Five groups encompass the sample age (Figure 21): from 20 years old or below; between 21 and 25 years old; between 26 and 30 years old; between 31 and 36 years old, and from 36 years old or above. Of the total sample, in the age group 2 there was 1 (6.7 per cent) respondent; in the age group 3 there were 9 (60 per cent) respondents; in the age group 4 there were 4 (26.7 per cent) respondents, and in the age group 5 there was 1 (6.7 per cent) respondent.

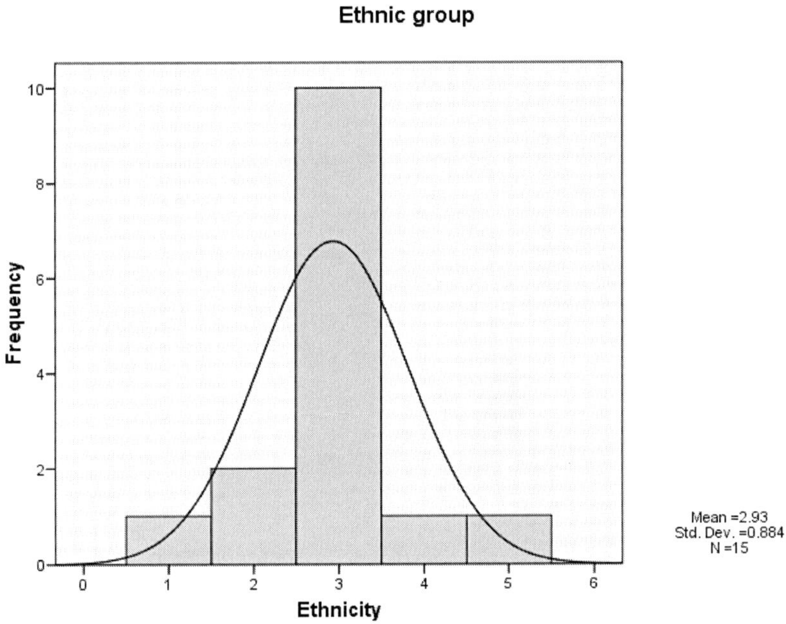

Figure 22: Ethnic groups

The ethnicity groups of the respondents are represented by (Figure 22) 1 (6.7 per cent) was: White (group 1); 2 (13.3 per cent) were Mixed (group 2); 10 (66.7 per cent) were Asian (group 3); 1 (6.7 per cent) was Black (group 4); and 1 (6.7 per cent) was Chinese (group 5). This classification was also used for classifying ethnicity in the 2001 UK Census.

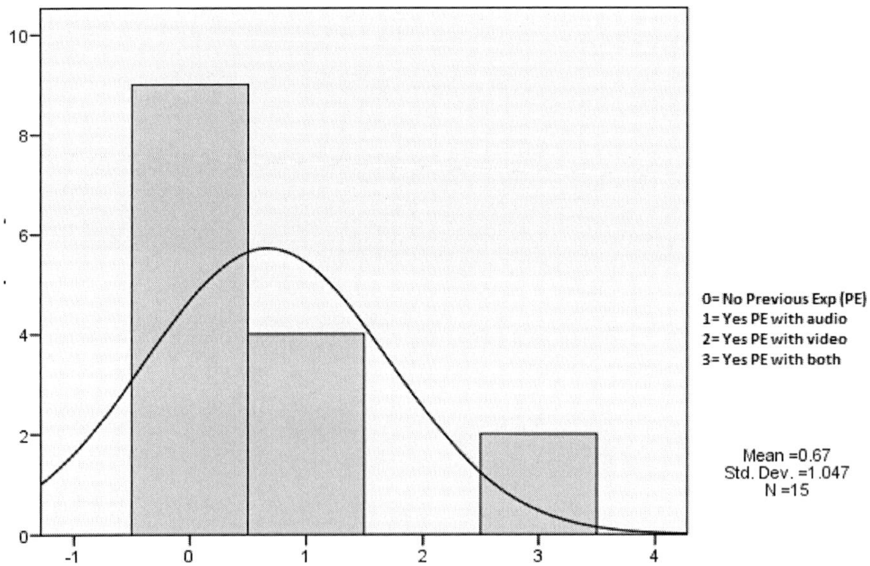

Figure 23: Question (1): Have you experienced audio or video feedback in the past?

The respondents who answered question (1), Have you experienced audio or video feedback in the past? (Figure 23): 9 (60 per cent) reported no previous experience with audio or video feedback in the past; 4 (26.7 per cent) reported having experience with audio feedback in the past; and 2 (13.3 per cent) reported having experience with both video and audio feedback. Nobody reported having only video feedback experience.

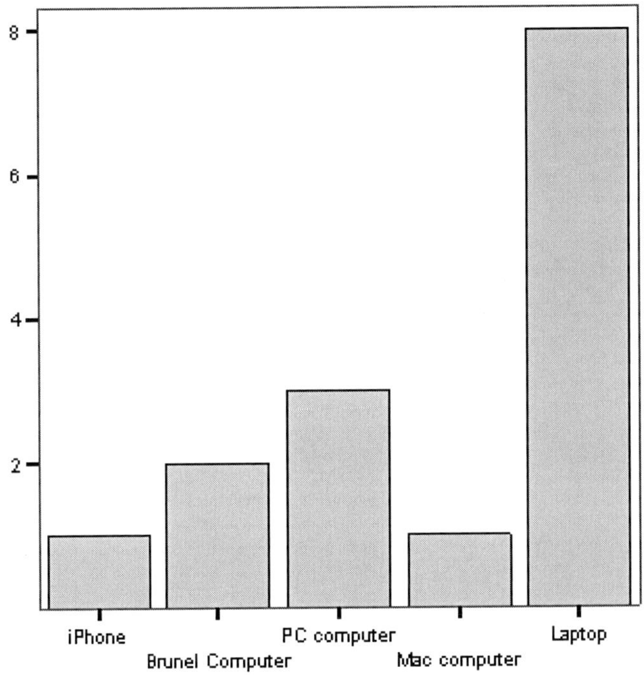

Figure 24: Question (2): What device you use to listen to your audio feedback on?

Regarding the respondents who answered question (2), What device you use to listen to your audio feedback on? (Figure 24): 1 (6.7 per cent) reported having used the iPhone to listen to the audio feedback; 2 (13.3 per cent) reported having used the Brunel computers to listen to the audio feedback; 3 (20 per cent) reported having used PC computers out of Brunel University to listen to the audio feedback; 1 (6.7 per cent) reported having used a Mac computer to listen to the audio feedback; and 8 (53.3 per cent) reported having used a laptop computer to listen to the audio feedback.

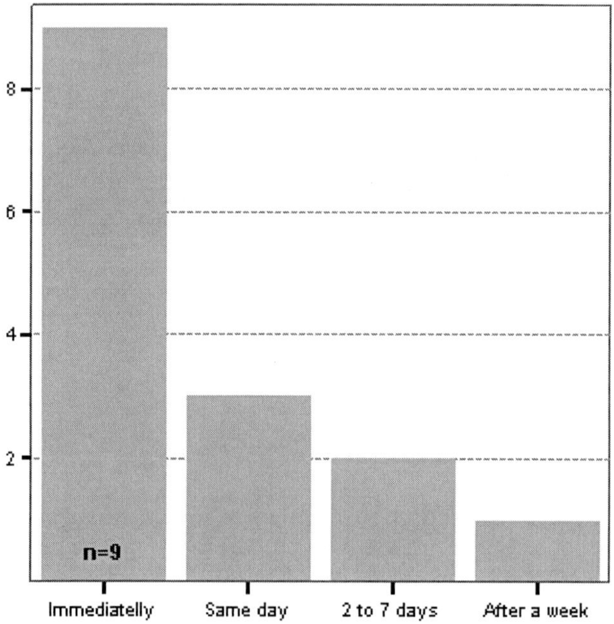

Figure 25: Question (3): How long did you wait before listening to it?

Of the respondents who answered question (3), How long after you received the audio feedback file did you wait before listening to it? (Figure 25): 9 (60 per cent) reported having listened to the audio feedback recording immediately; 3 (20 per cent) reported having listened to the audio feedback recording the same day; 2 (13.3 per cent) reported having listened to the audio feedback recording between 2 to 7 days later; and 1 (6.7 per cent) reported having listened to the audio feedback recording after a week.

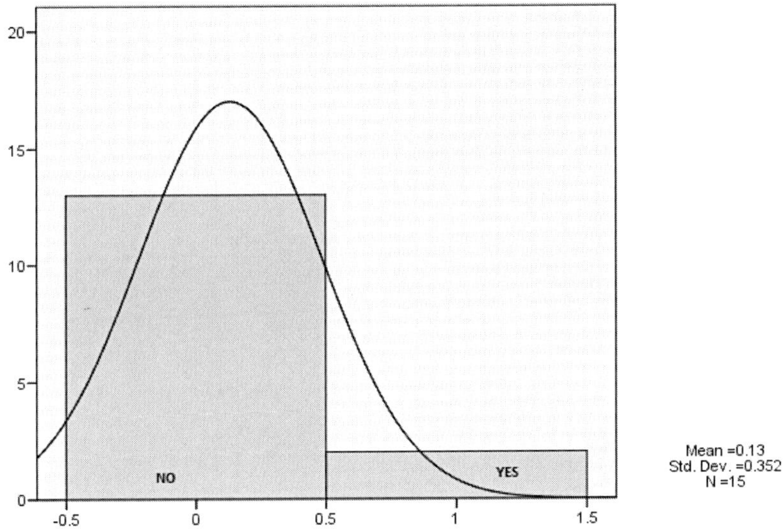

Figure 26: Question (4): Did you face any technical problems listening to the file?

Regarding the respondents who answered question (4), Did you face any technical problems listening to the audio feedback recording? (Figure 26): 13 (86.7 per cent) reported No; and 2 (13.3 per cent) reported Yes to having faced any technical problems listening to the audio feedback recording.

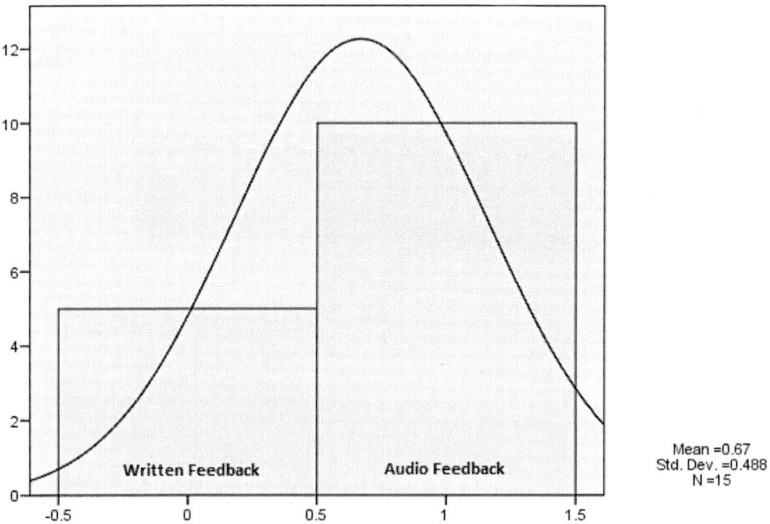

Figure 27: Question (5): Which form of feedback would you prefer?

Regarding the respondents who answered the question (5): Which form of feedback would you prefer? (Figure 27): 10 (66.7 per cent) reported having preferences for audio feedback; and 5 (33.3 per cent) reported having preferences for written feedback.

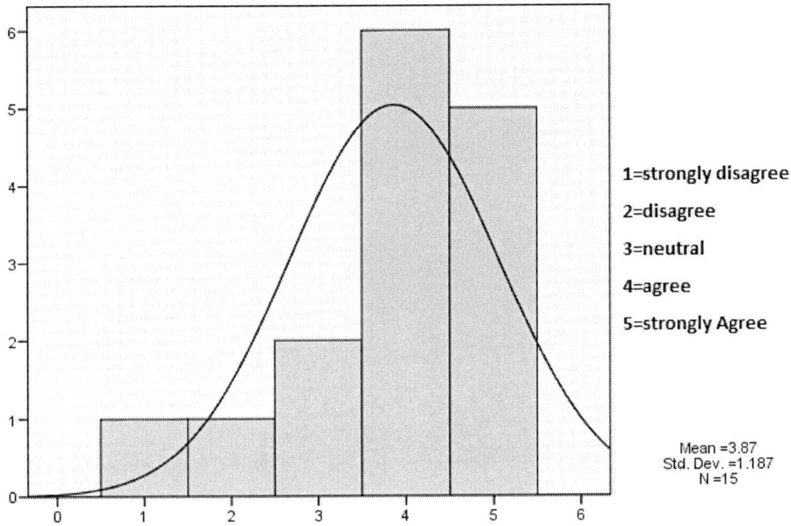

Figure 28: Question (6): I found the use of audio feedback accessible?

Regarding the respondents who answered question (6), I found the use of audio feedback accessible? (Figure 28):

1 (6.7 per cent) reported strongly disagree with the statement;
1 (6.7 per cent) reported disagree with the statement;
2 (13.3 per cent) reported neutral with the statement;
6 (40 per cent) reported agree with the statement;
5 (33.3 per cent) reported strongly agree with the statement.

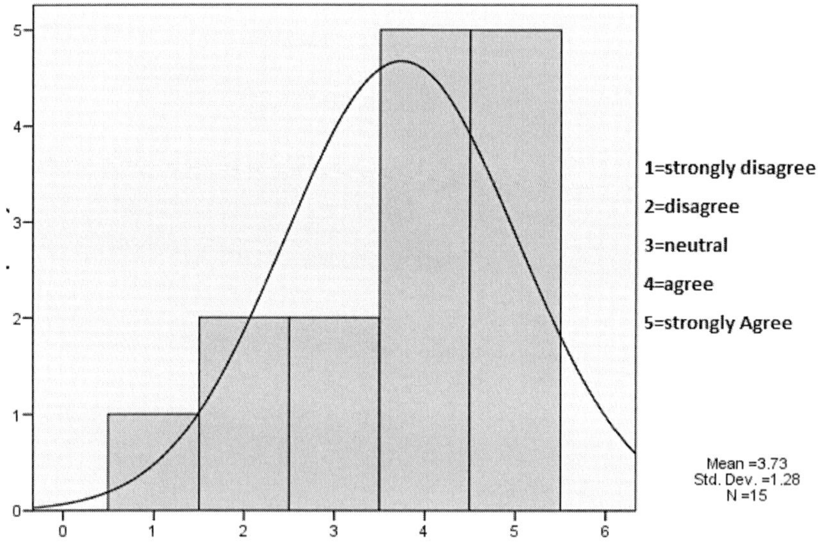

Figure 29: Question (7): I found the use of audio feedback a valuable contribution?

Next, of the respondents who answered question (7), I found the use of audio feedback a valuable contribution? (Figure 29):

1 (6.7 per cent) reported strongly disagree with the statement;
2 (13.3 per cent) reported disagree with the statement;
2 (13.3 per cent) reported neutral with the statement;
5 (33.3 per cent) reported agree with the statement;
5 (33.3 per cent) reported strongly agree with the statement.

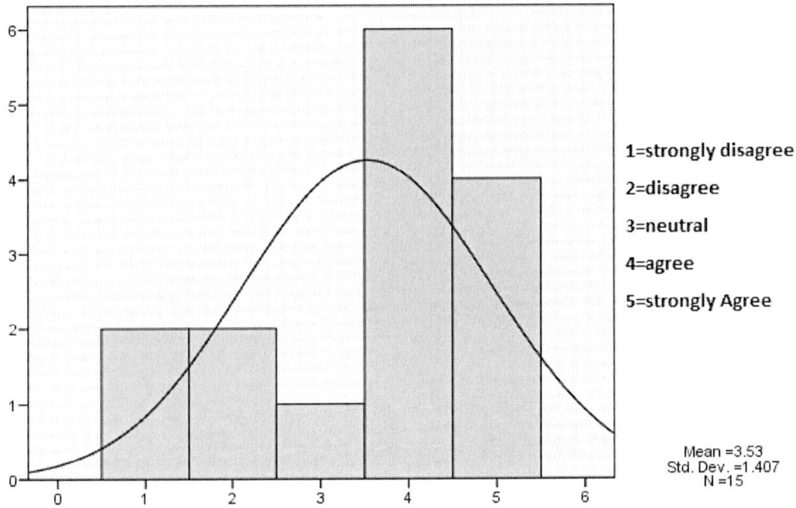

Figure 30: Question (8): I would like to see continued use for my coursework?

Next, of the respondents who answered question (8), I would like to see continued use of audio feedback for my coursework? (Figure 30):

2 (13.3 per cent) reported strongly disagree with the statement;
2 (13.3 per cent) reported disagree with the statement;
1 (6.7 per cent) reported neutral with the statement;
6 (40 per cent) reported agree with the statement;
4 (26.7 per cent) reported strongly agree with the statement.

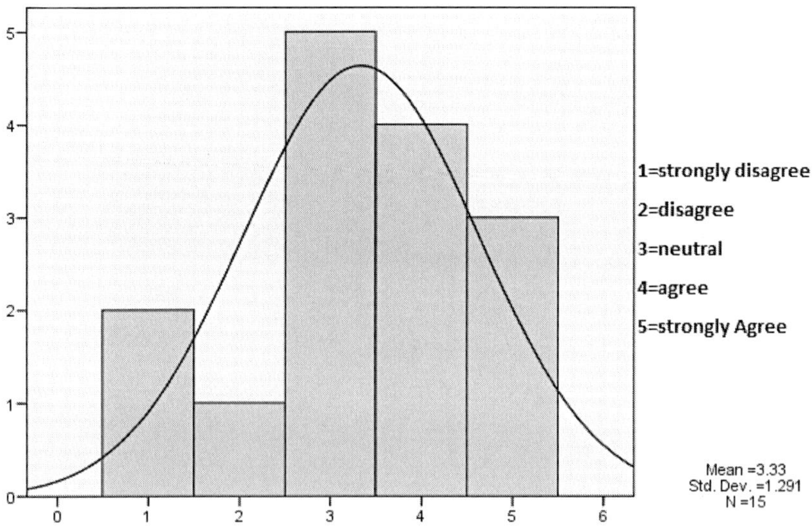

Figure 31: Question (9): I found the use of audio feedback contributed to my learning?

Next, of the respondents who answered question (9), I found the use of audio feedback contributed to my learning? (Figure 31):

2 (13.3 per cent) reported strongly disagree with the statement;
1 (6.7 per cent) reported disagree with the statement;
5 (33.3 per cent) reported neutral with the statement;
4 (26.7 per cent) reported agree with the statement;
3 (20 per cent) reported strongly agree with the statement.

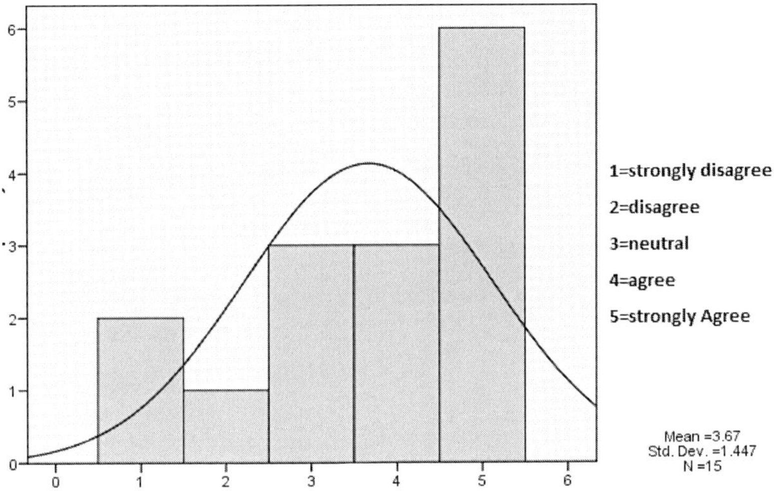

Figure 32: Question (10): I would like audio feedback used for other courses?

Next, of the respondents who answered question (10), I would like to see audio feedback used for other courses at Brunel? (Figure 32):

2 (13.3 per cent) reported strongly disagree with the statement;
1 (6.7 per cent) reported disagree with the statement;
3 (20 per cent) reported neutral with the statement;
3 (20 per cent) reported agree with the statement;
6 (40 per cent) reported strongly agree with the statement.

5.4.4 Discussion

The opinions of students collected for this study are favourable to the use of interactive audio feedback for final assignments.

The majority of the students had no previous experience of audio feedback. It can be considered favourable because it helps to avoid any confounding effect being introduced into the study by a third variable (Clark, 1983). The device that was most often used to listen to the audio feedback was the laptop, even though personal PCs or university PCs were available on campus. It makes perfect sense if we consider that a laptop is the more immediate computer device to an MBA student. The tendency was to listen to the audio feedback immediately (60 per cent), or the same day (80 per cent), after it was received. Few expressed any technical difficulties in downloading and listening to the audio files. Most simply clicked on the link and the file opened in Windows Media Player. The only reported downside of audio feedback (from the students' perspective) was that it was more difficult to navigate and focus on specific aspects.

Number of participants (N)– 15	**mean**	**SD**
Audio feedback found **accessible** (Likert scale 1 to 5)	3.87	1.187
Audio feedback a **valuable contribution** (Likert scale 1 to 5)	3.73	1.280
Will like **use** of audio feedback for **my coursework** (Likert scale 1 to 5)	3.53	1.407
Audio feedback **contributed to my learning** (Likert scale 1 to 5)	3.33	1.291
Audio feedback **used for other courses** at Brunel (Likert scale 1 to 5)	3.67	1.447

Table 5: Experiment 3 Students' opinions about the use of audio feedback

A majority considered audio feedback to be accessible, and to be a valuable contribution to teaching and learning (see Table 3). It is expected to be used as a feedback mechanism in other coursework and courses in Brunel University. The results provide support for the quality enhancement hypothesis H2.

5.5 Experiment Four

5.5.1 Method

5.5.1.1 Participants

The subject is a male Senior Academic Practice Adviser in the Staff Development Unit at Brunel University in West London, UK. The Unit provides support to probationary members of the academic staff in their academic role, helps in settling within the Brunel and the wider HE community, and helps with personal commitments to achieving personal and organizational expectations.

Audio Feedback for Oral/Poster Presentation

Luis Palacios (cbpglpp@brunel.ac.uk)

The purpose of this survey is to identify the effectiveness of Audio feedback within an Oral/Poster presentation context

Date:	**Native Language**
Module	**Gender**
Age	**Country of origin**

1. Have you experienced audio or video feedback in the past (tick one only)??
   Audio ____
   Video ____
   Both ____
   No ____

2. What device you use to listen your audio feedback?
   a. i-phone ____
   b. Brunel computer ____
   c. PC computer ____
   d. Mac computer ____
   e. Laptop ____
   f. Blackberry ____
   h. other (__________) ____

3. How long after you received the audio feedback file did you wait before listening to it (tick one only)??
   a. immediately ____
   b. same day ____
   c. Next day ____
   d. 2 to 7 day ____
   e. after a week ____

4. Did you face any technical problems listening to the file? Yes____ No____
If yes, please specify____

5. Which form of feedback would you prefer (tick one only)?
   Audio ____
   Written ____

	Strongly disagree	Disagree	Neutral	Agree	Strongly agree
6. "I found the use of audio feedback accessible"					
7. "I found the use of audio feedback a valuable contribution					
8. "I would like to see continued use of audio feedback for my coursework"					
9. "I found the use of audio feedback contributed to my learning "					
10. "I would like to see audio feedback used for other courses at Brunel"					
11. "I consider audio feedback deliver the message more accurately than written feedback"					
12. "Audio feedback is more personalised than writing feedback "					

Figure 33: Experiment 4- Questionnaire to capture presenter opinion

Professional Development in Academic Practice

Programme of Development in Academic Practice
(PDAP)
ORAL PRESENTATION

Brunel UNIVERSITY LONDON

Presenter's Name: **Date:**
School/Unit:

1 - unsatisfactory, 2 - satisfactory, 3 - impressive, 4 - outstanding

Criteria	**1**	**2**	**3**	**4**	**Comments** Identify particular strengths and suggestions for improvement
Presentation is Clear: e.g., audibility, pace, fluency, body language, eye contact					
Presentation is Engaging: e.g., suitable balance of oral and visual resource, interesting topic, appropriate to audience					
Content is Informative: e.g., well organised, cohesive, focused, relevant to audience					
Presentation is Original or Innovative: e.g. original research, innovative approach to research or presentation					

For PDAP Staff Only - Outcome: Pass / Needs Further Work [Circle as appropriate]
Moderator [Signature]: **Date:**

[Name printed]:

NB: A Pass is conditional until approved by the Moderation Board

Figure 34: Experiment 4- Template to guide the evaluation of the oral presentation

He is using a guiding template (Figure 34 and Figure 35), with notes taken from oral/poster presentations given as final assignments by new or probationary members of Brunel academic staff taking the "Programme of Development in Academic Practice" (PDAP) teaching course. The PDAP programme is designed specifically to meet the professional development needs of probationary members of the academic staff at Brunel University.

The Professional Development in Academic Practice programme is accredited by the Higher Education Academy, and on completion provides eligibility for recognition as Fellow of the Higher Education Academy.

5.5.1.2 Materials and apparatus

Audio feedback (speech) was recorded as a mp3 file using Audacity audio software installed on a Sony VAIO VGN-FS115B laptop using Windows XP. Text feedback was recorded (typed) using Microsoft Word 2007 on the same Sony VAIO VGN-FS115B. It was stored as a Word .docx file.

The previous questionnaire (Figure 19) was redesigned to produce a new improved version (Figure 33) to capture the opinions of the lecturer and students, and to identify the effectiveness of audio feedback in these final presentation assignments.

In addition, the lecturer used a template that guides the assessment of the main areas to be taken into consideration.

The template helps the process to take notes from final oral presentation assignments on new or probationary members of Brunel academic staff.

The notes used by the lecturer evaluating the presentation to produce the feedback were created following four main criteria: clarity of the presentation, e.g. audibility, pace, fluency, body language, eye contact; engaging, e.g. suitable balance of oral and visual resources, interesting topic, appropriate to audience; informative, e.g. well organized, cohesive, focused, relevant to audience; and originality or innovative, e.g. original research, innovative approach to research or presentation (see Figure 34: Experiment 4- Template to guide the evaluation of the oral presentation, and Figure 35).

Programme of Development in Academic Practice
(PDAP)
POSTER

Brunel UNIVERSITY LONDON

Presenter's Name: **Date:**
School/Unit:

1 - unsatisfactory, 2 - satisfactory, 3 - impressive, 4 - outstanding

<u>Criteria</u>	1	2	3	4	**Comments** Identify particular strengths and suggestions for improvement
Presentation of information <u>on the Poster itself</u> is Clear e.g. clear to read, data easily comprehensible, appropriate use of colour for clarity					
Poster is Visually Interesting: e.g. not simply chunks of text or numerous tables, colour/images used to attract the eye					
Content <u>of the Poster</u> is Informative: e.g. properly referenced, clear development of ideas, conclusions are apparent					
The Poster is Original/ Innovative: e.g. in terms of original/innovative research and/or how it is presented on the poster					

For PDAP Staff Only - Outcome: Pass / Needs Further Work [Circle as appropriate]
Moderator [Signature]: **Date:**

[Name printed]:

<u>**NB**</u>: A Pass is conditional until approved by the Moderation Board

Figure 35: Experiment 4- Template to guide the evaluation of the poster presentation

The questionnaire structure encompasses three main areas. An initial area that requires demographic information such date of birth, native language, age, gender and country of origin, for example.

Date:__ Module___ Native Language___ Age_ Gender: M_ F_ Country of origin: ____

A second area that focuses on previous experience, devices used and the technical difficulties faced and initial attitude before or at the moment the students have received the feedback.

5. Which form of feedback would you prefer (tick one only)?
Audio ____
Written ____

Then, a final area that evaluates student opinion after feedback has been received. A Likert scale is introduced in these question areas to evaluate accessibility of the feedback, if it is considered a valuable contribution, a contribution to learning, and the students' expectations about use audio feedback in other courses, or coursework for example

"I found the use of audio feedback contributed to my learning":
a. Strongly Disagree ____
b. Disagree ____
c. Neutral ____
d. Agree ____
e. Strongly agree ____

It was designed to determine the experience and tools used when the feedback was listened to. The questionnaire also investigates accessibility to the audio file, how valuable the students consider the audio feedback, the contribution to the students' learning, and their interest in using the audio feedback in the future in other courses.

5.5.2 Procedure

In experiment three, the conditions were kept the same as in experiment two ("A" for audio and "T" for text), but the procedures have slightly changed including different participants and materials. The introduction of a template that guides the production of feedback is one of the main factors considered in this approach.

A random sample of eight finals guiding template (Figure 34 and Figure 35) with notes taken from oral/poster presentations templates were divided into two groups.

The first group of four evaluations were used for the T condition. For each evaluation, the start time was recorded at the moment where typing began, and the end time at the moment where typing was completed as indicated by the tutor. There was no reading time prior to commencement of typing. This requirement was different than in experiment 2. However, reading time of the evaluation report during the construction of feedback was included.

For the A condition, again the start time was recorded at the moment the Audacity recording button was first clicked on, and the end time at the moment where the Audacity recording button was clicked off as indicated by the tutor. The tutor was not permitted to pause the recording button. This is also different than in experiment 2. The thinking/reading time was included in the overall time. Immediately after the feedback recording finished, the tutor was interviewed. Then, audio files and a feedback survey were delivered by email to the students to collect their experiences.

5.5.3 Results

In experiment 4, the average time taken to produce the text feedback was 6.8 min, and to produce the audio feedback was 2.5 min (see Table 7). The Shapiro-Wilk test for Normality that is more appropriate for the small sample sizes (< 50 samples) of the data was applied to indicate the normality of the data.

	group	Shapiro-Wilk		
		Statistic	df	Sig.
Feedback	T	.723	4	.021*
	A	.843	4	.206*

*p < .05; ES = 2.02

Table 6: Experiment 4- The Shapiro-Wilk test for Normality

We can see from the above table that for the "A" and "T" Feedback condition the dependent variable "Time" was normally distributed.

There is a reduction from the time taken to create the text feedback to the time taken to create the audio feedback of around 63 per cent (mean difference = -257 s or 4:17 min).

Unpaired Student's t-test, t(6) = -3.801, p < .05, with an effect size of 2.88.

Group	Recording Time/s	
	M	*SD*
T (n-4)	416.25	123.82
A (n=4)	158.75	54.97

**p < .05; ES = 2.88*

Table 7: Experiment 4- Feedback Recording Times (in seconds)

The tutor considers that one of the main reasons for using audio rather than text feedback is related to the popularity that the use of audio feedback is having in the industry. There were concerns about the mistakes that could be produced while developing the audio feedback. However, the tutor created a mental structure to follow while developing the audio feedback to keep consistency among all of them. However, he recognised that some mistakes were made while following this mental structure, e.g. not highlighting that the participant had not been told that they had passed the exercise, but they were reduced with practice. The tutor found the exercise "pretty tiring and would probably do this again in a more relaxed context such as at home". It may be because of the intensity of trying to ensure that he was speaking clearly and leaving nothing out. The tutor felt more confident using Audacity indicating that it was "far easier to use than podcasting software such as Camtasia, which he found very difficult to pause". However, he is not sure how the students will react to the introduction of this new approach. The tutor is very enthusiastic about the idea of using audio feedback on real courses.

The results from the students' survey are presented below. The sample (N = 4) of new staff participating in the programme in development of academic practice was composed of four males. Five groups encompass the sample age from 20 years old or below; between 21 and 25 years old; between 26 and 30 years old; between 31 and 36 years old, and from 36 years old or above. All the respondents in age group 5 were 36 or over.

The ethnicity groups of the respondents is represented by 5 groups as follows: White (group 1), Mixed (group 2), Asian (group 3), Black (group 4), and Chinese (group 5). The respondents belong to the ethnicity groups 1 and 5 in the following proportion: 50 per cent White and 50 per cent Chinese.

Of the respondents who answered question (1), Have you experienced audio or video feedback in the past?, all 4 (100 per cent) reported no previous experience with audio or video feedback.

Regarding the respondents who answered question (2), What device do you use to listen to your audio feedback?: 2 (50 per cent) reported having used the Bruncl computers to listen to the audio feedback; 1 (25 per cent) reported having used a Mac computer to listen to the audio feedback; and 1 (25 per cent) reported having used a laptop to listen to the audio feedback.

Of the respondents who answered question (3), How long after you received the audio feedback file did you wait before listening to it?: 3 (75 per cent) reported having listened to the audio feedback recording immediately; and 1 (25 per cent) reported having listened to the audio feedback recording the same day.

Next, of the respondents who answered question (4), Did you face any technical problems listening to the audio feedback recording?: all respondents (100 per cent) reported not having faced any technical problems listening to the audio feedback recording.

Regarding the respondents who answered question (5), Which form of feedback would you prefer?: 3 (75 per cent) reported having preferences for audio feedback; and 1 (25 per cent) reported having preferences for written feedback.

Regarding the respondents who answered question (6), I found the use of audio feedback accessible?: 1 respondent (25 per cent) agreed with the statement; and 3 (75 per cent) strongly agreed with the statement.

Next, of the respondents who answered question (7), I found the use of audio feedback a valuable contribution?: 2 (50 per cent) agreed with the statement; and 2 (50 per cent) strongly agreed with the statement.

Next, of the respondents who answered question (8), I would like to see continued use of audio feedback for my coursework?:

2 (50 per cent) were neutral about the statement;
1 (25 per cent) agreed with the statement; and
1 (25.7 per cent) strongly agreed with the statement.

Next, of the respondents who answered question (9): I found the use of audio feedback contributed to my learning? (Figure 31)

2 (13.3 per cent) strongly disagreed with the statement;
1 (6.7 per cent) disagreed with the statement;

5 (33.3 per cent) were neutral about the statement;
4 (26.7 per cent) agreed with the statement; and
3 (20 per cent) strongly agreed with the statement.

Next, of the respondents who answered the question (10), I would like to see audio feedback used for other courses at Brunel?:

1 (25 per cent) disagreed with the statement;
2 (50 per cent) were neutral about the statement; and
1 (25 per cent) strongly agreed with the statement.

Next, of the respondents who answered question (11).,I consider audio feedback delivers the message more accurately than written feedback?:

2 (50 per cent) disagreed with the statement;
1 (25 per cent) were neutral about the statement; and
1 (25 per cent) agreed with the statement.

Next, of the respondents who answered question (12), Audio feedback is more personalized than written feedback?:

3 (75 per cent) were neutral about the statement; and
1 (25 per cent) agreed with the statement.

5.5.4 Discussion

This study also reiterated that the process of creating feedback is reduced by using audio feedback by 63 per cent. In addition, the reduction in time is increased in this experiment compared to the previous one. When comparing experiments two and three in this regard, it indicates that the time taken to produce the audio feedback is even less (from a reduction of 40 per cent to 63 per cent). This suggests that the template guidance introduced to facilitate the development of the feedback is having a positive effect on the production of interactive audio feedback.

When interviewed, the tutor reported that he felt more comfortable working with audio than text feedback.

He particularly appreciated the increase in the recording rate facilitated by audio. He reported that he had erroneously expected the creation and uploading of MP3 files to be much more complex than it turned out to be.

The students' perceptions praised the audio feedback for feeling "extremely personal" and "less abstract than written text".

None of the students expressed any technical difficulties in downloading and listening to the audio files. Most simply clicked on the link and the file opened in Windows Media Player.

The only reported downside of audio feedback (from the students' perspective) was that it was more difficult to scan and focus on particular aspects. However most believed this was more than compensated for by the richness of audio feedback.

5.6 Chapter Discussion

The studies suggest that audio recording can decrease the time it takes to create feedback by 40-63 per cent. There are significant differences in the production of audio versus written feedback. In experiment 2, the mean difference of -199 s (3:19 min) is statistically reliable, with Unpaired Student's *t*-test, $t(6) = -2.854$, one-tailed, $p < .05$, with an effect size of 2.02 (small). In experiment 4, the time taken to create the audio feedback was 63 per cent (mean difference = -257 s or 4:17 min) with Unpaired Student's *t*-test, $t(6) = -3.801$, $p < .05$, with an effect size of 2.88. There is an increase in the reduction of the time between the two experiments (production time of the audio feedback in experiment 4 is less) that seems to be related to the introduction of the guiding template (Figure 34 and Figure 35) that directs the procedure of taking notes when evaluating the presentations. These results allow us to conclude that the interactive features of technology have generated a sort of speeding effect in the production of feedback.

Interactivity, as indicated in **MISSING**, when implemented in an e-learning system provides the capability for the system to react immediately and reciprocally to the learner input. Thus, the lecturer speeds up the production of the audio feedback, cutting down the time that is usually required to produce it. Moreover, the effect is also related to the intrinsic nature of audio when compared to typing, as explained in the literature review (see **MISSING**). In several studies, researchers found evidence that suggest that oral skills require less cognitive processing than writing.

Tutors reported that there was a significant time saving in the process of creating the feedback. All tutors producing feedback preferred recording audio feedback because the speaking is a more "natural" and effortless process than typing. There was concern about the mistakes that could be produced while developing the audio feedback. However, all tutors created a mental structure to follow while developing the audio feedback to keep consistency among all of the audio feedbacks. They feel positive about the use of this methodology. None of the students expressed any technical difficulties in downloading and listening to the audio files. Most simply clicked on the link and the file opened in Windows Media Player. The study assumed that the quantity of feedback was similar for each mode (audio or text). Indeed, tutors were asked to attempt to ensure this.

The key aspects that participants valued in audio feedback were: audio is more detailed because it carries more information; it seems to create a more personal and closer relationship; and the understanding of the feedback is not corrupted by poor typing. It implies that there is a communicational effect in the use of interactivity to deliver the audio feedback.

CHAPTER SIX

INTERACTIVE TEXTING FEEDBACK

6.1 Introduction

Brunel is one of a number of British universities created in the 1960s following the Robbins Report on higher education that recommended the immediate expansion of universities. In 1995 the University expanded again, which increased the number of courses that it was able to offer, and the size of the student body increased to over 12,000. This dramatic expansion in recent years makes it increasingly difficult for all students to physically attend a lecture, at a particular time and place. Pedagogically speaking it is also not appropriate to deliver lessons using traditional methods to these large audiences. An alternative mechanism using technology named Interactive Texting Feedback (ITF) has therefore been envisaged to enhance and verify that the teaching is reaching the students. It will engage the learners in these large courses with the lecturer in order to experience a certain degree of interactivity. ITF is a pedagogical approach to providing formative feedback to a student audience using SMS, often called text messaging.

ITF adds another technological resource to the teacher's arsenal, combining technology and pedagogical strategies to improve the learning experience. Interactive feedback as used in this research is information sent back to the student to modify his or her thinking or behaviour in order to improve their learning (Shute, 2008). Immediate constructive feedback offers a valuable contribution to the learning experience, because it helps to identify misconceptions and create mental schemata that can be added to existing knowledge to form new skills or attitudes.

There is a four-step pedagogical procedure in the process of using ITF: question, answer, response collection and feedback discussion. The procedure is based on the interaction model described in section 2.5. The lecturer poses a *question* to the audience after teaching a lesson to determine the level of understanding of the material presented. Technology is used to display the information, e.g. Microsoft PowerPoint, whiteboard, etc., and eliciting a cognitive process (**initiation**). Then, the students *answer* by sending a SMS message using their mobile phones to a SMS voting polls system (**response**). At this stage students just reply with a SMS text message indicating the letter that identifies the correct answer to the question. The system *collects* and processes the *responses*. Next, the students receive immediate *feedback* about the presented material that elicits a pedagogical discussion (**feedback**). The results are displayed in real time. The constructive feedback based on the student's response is used by the lecturer to facilitate discussion and provide guidance.

A good voting system, whether electronic or using traditional paper ballots, is characterised (Kohno, 2004) by anonymity, tamper-resistance, comprehensibility and usability by the entire voting population (human factors criteria). ITF complies with these features. Anonymity is guaranteed, since the process is performed automatically with no intervention from the lecturer. Security is based on compiled algorithms generated by the system. It used HTML to easily integrate into a company or personal website where the system generates a short JavaScript code that is simple to integrate. It is very simple to use, due to the fact that almost everybody has a mobile phone. A normal network charge applies when voting using a mobile phone, and since there are no entirely free SMS polls they are less likely to be abused.

The mobile phone is an important piece of technology, and the surrounding pedagogical framework (Sharples, Taylor & Vavoula, 2005) employed. Learning mediated by mobile devices assists the learners in their goals of transforming their knowledge and skills by engagement and use of contemporary practices that enable effective learning. These practices, according to Sharples (2005), emphasise the following aspects: a learner-centred approach that enables the student to reason based on his or her own experience; a knowledge-centred approach that focuses on a curriculum built from sound foundations on validated knowledge; and an assessment-centred approach that provides constructive feedback.

SMS usages are increasing in education (Stone, Briggs & Smith, 2002). Research implemented to test the effectiveness of a two-way SMS campaign for a UK youth brand demonstrated that participants were motivated to participate and were able to perform complex tasks using their mobile phones. Complexity was achieved by requesting users to perform a series of interactive SMS exchanges to achieve completion of a task or goal. There are economical and educational motivations for this research. The size of undergraduate classes in the business school is too big to be pedagogically appropriate. On the other hand, there are assurances that learning is achieved using the correct methodology.

The Interactive Texting Feedback study is related to the mediator system in the pedagogical triangle. The methodologies used focus on determining the effectiveness of interactivity in this context. It responds to the final experimental hypothesis in this research that Interactive Texting Feedback is an effective approach to enhancing learning practice. The following study was designed to confirm the experimental hypothesis.

6.2 Experiment

6.2.1 Method

6.2.1.1 Participants

The participants were two groups of 49 and 65 undergraduate and postgraduate students in marketing courses at the Business School at Brunel University in London, UK. Their age ranged between 18 and 30 years old, and they were from different ethnic backgrounds.

6.2.1.2 Materials and apparatus

There are four technological components used in this experiment: mobile devices, a Viglen computer using PowerPoint with access to the Internet, a projector, and the "Cardboard Fish" SMS poll service. The mobile phones were the personal devices of the students who voluntarily agreed to participate in the experiment (they were from different brands and operators). They were used to send SMS messages to the Cardboard Fish central system. The PC was a normal computer with access to the Internet that was employed to display a PowerPoint presentation and provide access to the Cardboard Fish SMS polls tool. It also interacted with the projector to magnify the display onto the bigger screen of the classroom. The Cardboard Fish SMS polls tool allows the setting up of voting polls and displaying the results on any website. Normal network charges apply when voting. Anybody can sign up for a free account to use the Webmaster SMS tools and some other services by going to http://webmastersms.cardboardfish.com. Registration is required by giving some essential basic information such as contact name, username, password, e-mail address. With the SMS Poll application you can allow visitors to the website to vote in polls by simply sending a SMS message. The lecturer can set up and administer the poll options, and the results will be displayed on the website for all visitors to see. The poll offers up to 26 options at once and it is fully customizable using cascading style sheets

Interactive Texting Survey (MG1016)

Luis Palacios (Luis.Palacios@brunel.ac.uk)

The purpose of this survey is to get your opinion about the effectiveness of interactive SMS texting with the view to the possibility of using it again later.

Date:_________Module________Level___________Age___Gender:M__F __Country :__________

1. Do you have a mobile phone?
   Yes____ No____ if *yes* indicate the make of your mobile phone____________________________

2. Who is your telecom service Provider?

a. T-Mobile	b.Vodafone	c. O2
d. Orange	e. Virgin	f. Other

3. How many free texts do you get per month on your current plan?
   a. 0 ____ d. 601- 900 ____
   b. 1- 300 ____ e. more than 900 ____
   c. 301- 600 ____

4. I would be willing to use some of my texts to participate in a lesson
   a. Strongly disagree ____ d. Agree ____
   b. Disagree ____ e. Strongly agree____
   c. Neutral ____

5. If I have more free texts, I will be more willing to participate in a lesson
   a. Strongly disagree ____ d. Agree ____
   b. Disagree ____ e. Strongly agree____
   c. Neutral ____

6. Did you have sufficient signal reception on your mobile phone in the classroom for SMS texting?
   Yes____ No____

7. When interactive SMS texting was used in the lab, did you participate in sending texts?
   Yes____ No____

8. How many texts would you be willing to use during a talk?
   a. 0 ____
   b. 1 - 3 ____
   c. 4- 7 ____
   d. 8 - 15 ____
   e. more than 15 ____

9. "I found the use of interactive SMS texting entertaining"
   a. Strongly disagree ____ d. Agree ____
   b. Disagree ____ e. Strongly agree____
   c. Neutral ____

10. "I found the use of interactive SMS texting contributed to my learning"
   a. Strongly disagree ____ d. Agree ____
   b. Disagree ____ e. Strongly agree____
   c. Neutral ____

11. "I would like to see continued use interactive SMS texting in my lectures"
   a. Strongly disagree ____ d. Agree ____
   b. Disagree ____ e. Strongly agree____
   c. Neutral ____

12. "I found the use of interactive SMS texting a valuable contribution"
   a. Strongly disagree ____ d. Agree ____
   b. Disagree ____ e. Strongly agree____

Figure 36: Interactive Texting Survey

(CSS) to change the colours, fonts, borders and other elements of the webmaster SMS applications. CSS is a style sheet language used for describing the presentation semantics (the look and formatting) of a document written in a mark-up language (Pfaffenberge et al., 2004).

A questionnaire was developed to capture the students' opinions. It contained twelve questions (see Figure 36) regarding demographic data, service provider, signal strength, SMS texts students receive from their service provider, how many they were willing to use in the experiment, and students' attitudes about the use of the pedagogical approach.

6.2.2 Procedure

The experiment design consists in the lecturer using the four-step pedagogical procedure mentioned in the introduction: question elicitation, students' answers, response collection gathering process for displaying the data, and finally a pedagogical process of discussion about the feedback is initiated.

The process starts when a question is presented to the audience after teaching a lesson (Figure 37). The question is related to the Marketing subject previously taught. These courses are designed for either those wishing to become marketing professionals (undergraduates) or others seeking a master's qualification in Marketing. The question is displayed using PowerPoint, and projected on the main board of the classroom where everybody can see it. The question usually follows a multiple-choice format with a "key" (right answer) and distracters to put students into a thoughtful state. Distracters are the incorrect answers presented as a choice in a multiple-choice test (Palacios & Evans, 2010b).

Then, students (Figure 38, left) reply sending an SMS message using their mobile phones to a Cardboard Fish website that behaves like an electronic poll system. Students cast their votes by texting a keyword and the option letter of their choice. Students are charged the standard network rate to send texts to the service number. The website service does not charge any extra fees.

The website collects the responses sent by the students and displays them using a customized template (Figure 38, right). The voting poll is easy to set up in any website because it automatically generates a short JavaScript code that can be inserted in the HTML source after the choices to be presented in the poll's interface are selected. Any messages sent to the poll system that do not contain a valid vote, count as spoiled votes. The spoiled votes can be identified by using administrator privileges offered to the manager of the account; also, you will be able to see a list of all current vote counts. Feedback is processed in real time. Therefore, the lecturer and the students can analyze the information almost immediately after the last answer has been sent.

Figure 37: First step: lecturer asking a question to the students

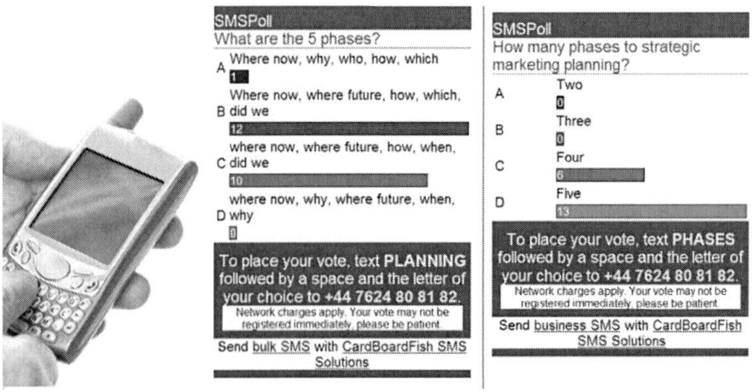

Figure 38: Second and third step: Student answers and data are collected

The lecturer facilitates a discussion and provides constructive feedback based on the students' responses. The lecturer can therefore easily channel the discussion to areas where he or she perceives the lesson was not understood. Students also get immediate feedback to clear up misconceptions.

6.2.3 Results

The information collected for the two groups (Table 8) indicates that the majority of the students have a mobile phone in the classroom. Only two in the Masters course and one in the Undergraduate course didn't have a mobile phone with them at the time of the experiment, but they all own one. We are therefore only taking into account students with their mobile phones in the class.

	Masters	Undergraduate
Number of participants (N)	65	49
Students with mobile ‘phones	64 (98 per cent)	45 (92 per cent)
Good signal	43 (66 per cent)	39 (78 per cent)
Willing to use texts	59 (91 per cent)	30 (61 per cent)

Table 8: Students participation by courses

Based on the information observed (Figure 39), the service provider with the best signal in the area is O2. We could also observe that students are willing to use up to a maximum of three text messages to participate. However, there is a decrease in this attitude when more messages are required.

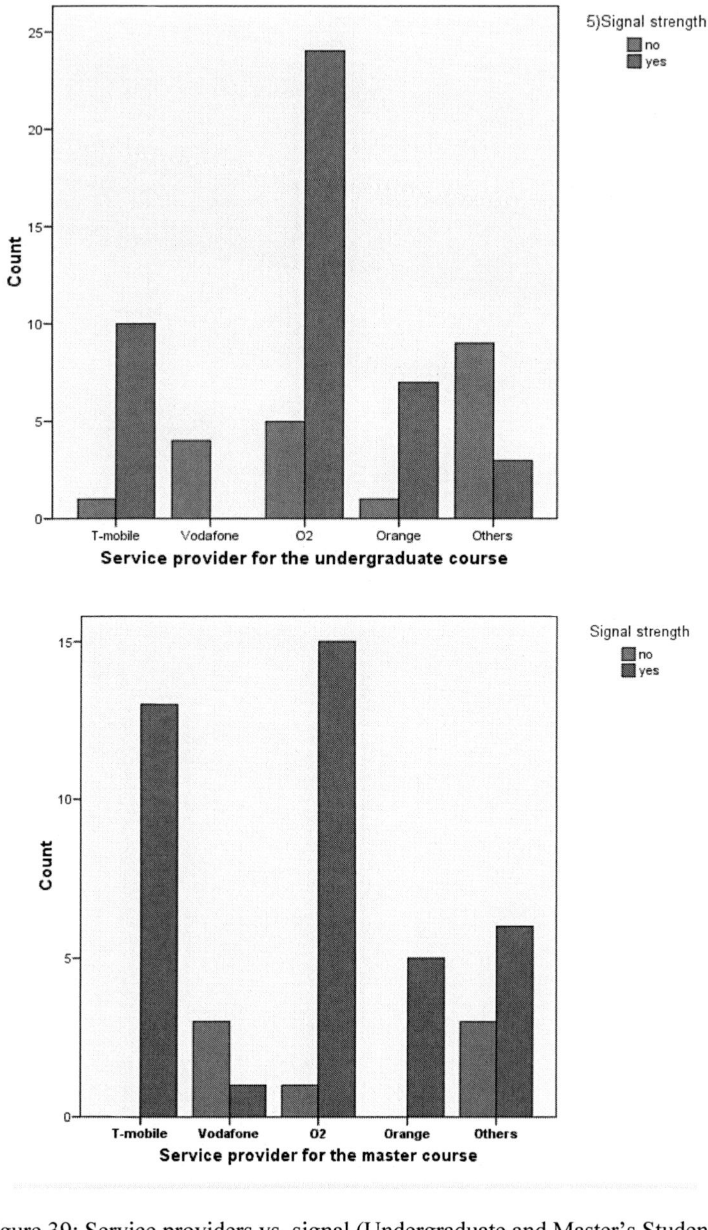

Figure 39: Service providers vs. signal (Undergraduate and Master's Students)

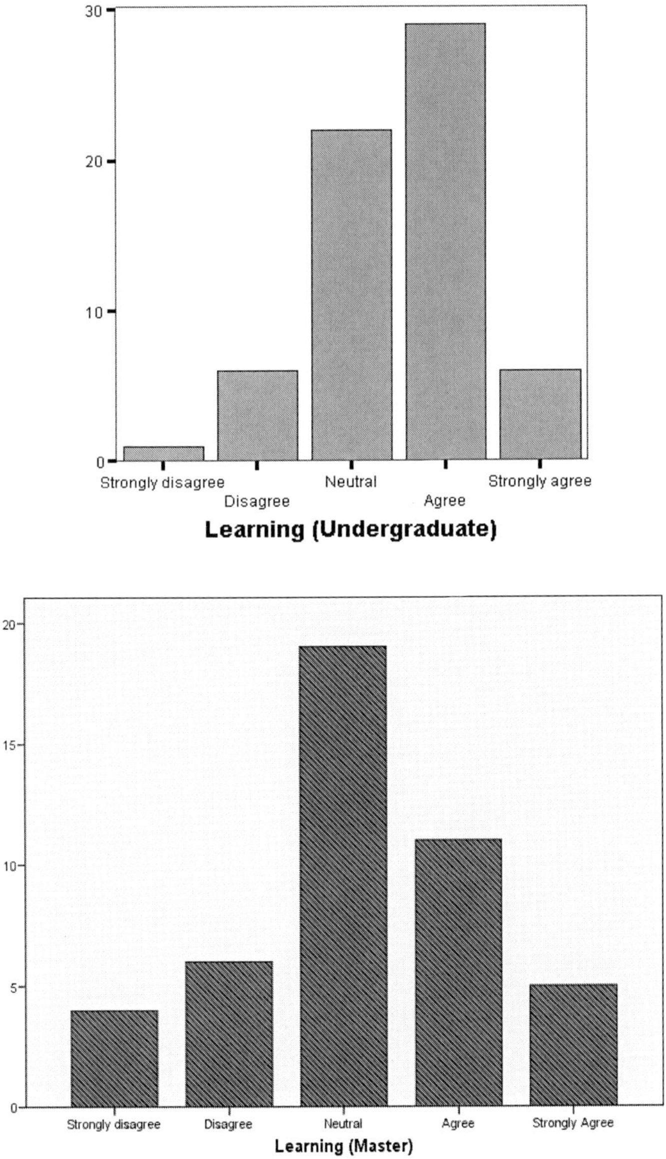

Figure 40: Contributed to learning using SMS (Undergraduate and Master's Students)

There is a positive attitude towards the use of this approach and students consider it as a valuable complement of the instruction as can be seen in Table 9.

Students seem to be more willing to use texts in the Undergraduate course (mean 2.3 (SD=1.5) than in the Master's course (mean1.5 SD=.9). However, Masters (mean 3.5 (SD=.7) consider that use of the system is valuable unlike Undergraduate students (mean 3.1 (SD=.9)

	Courses					
	Undergraduate			Masters		
	Mean	Std. Deviation	N	Mean	Std. Deviation	N
Entertainment	3.44	1.099	45	3.66	0.801	64
Contribute to Learning	3.16	1.086	45	3.52	0.854	64
Continuing using in class	3.00	0.977	45	3.55	0.775	64
Valuable Contribution	3.13	0.919	45	3.50	0.735	64
Spread to other modules	2.91	1.062	45	3.42	0.887	64

Table 9: Descriptive Statistics for the Undergraduate and Master's Courses

Pearson Correlation Sig. (2-tailed)= PC

	(E)		(CL)		(CU)		(VC)		(SM)	
PC	Master	Under	Master	Under	Master	Under	Master	Under	Master	Under
Entertainment (E)	1	1	.588 (**)	.531 (**)	.512 (**)	.572 (**)	.405 (**)	.637 (**)	.564 (**)	.716 (**)
Contribute to Learning (CL)	.588 (**)	.531 (**)	1	1	.598 (**)	.642 (**)	.620 (**)	.752 (**)	.588 (**)	.643 (**)
Continuing using in class(CU)	.512 (**)	.572 (**)	.598 (**)	.642 (**)	1	1	.544 (**)	.734 (**)	.698 (**)	.788 (**)
Valuable Contribution (VC)	**.405** (**)	**.637** (**)	.620 (**)	.752 (**)	.544 (**)	.734 (**)	1	1	.597 (**)	.780 (**)
Spread to other modules (SM)	**.564** (**)	**.716** (**)	.588 (**)	.643 (**)	.698 (**)	.788 (**)	.597 (**)	.780 (**)	1	1

Table 10: Correlations for both Undergraduate and Master's Course

Correlations among the variables relating to their attitude towards the system show it to be significant as can be seen from the correlation in Table 10.

6.3 Chapter Discussion

The object of this experiment was to determine whether interactive feedback using SMS is a valid and effective pedagogical approach to learning. ARS systems as mentioned in the literature review at **MISSING** have traditionally been used when managing large audiences but interactivity introduced by adding a very low cost approach allows the lecturer and the learner better comprehension of the educational material taught.

The results confirm student satisfaction and willingness to participate in present and future experiments. Inferential analysis demonstrates good correlation among the variables related to the service provider, signal strength and number of SMS texts students were willing to use. Significant results indicate that students consider the use of this approach as a viable contribution to learning, and it should spread to other modules in Brunel University.

It has been noticed that student intervention increased using this approach because of the anonymous nature of the SMS text sent. There is a communicational effect of this interactive system between the lecturer and the students. The lecturer can almost instantly determine whether his/her educational message has been delivered to the audience independently of the size of the classroom.

Similarly, it can be seen in the variables related to attitudes. This is a cost-effective approach to learning since it is a new educational strategy where the students receive immediate constructive feedback and it motivates them to react in real time to the lesson presented.

CHAPTER SEVEN

GENERAL DISCUSSION

This book examined the hypothesis that interactivity has a positive effect in enhancing the learning experience when used in an e-learning system. Interactivity has the ability to respond contingently to the learner's actions and is positioned as an important instrument for promoting learning (Beauchamp and Kennewell, 2010), but with little scientific evidence to sustain this idea. This position is reinforced by the penetration of technology that has increased worldwide at an exponential rate in the last decade (Chinn and Fairlie, 2010). Interactivity is notably associated with technology because of the unlimited capability of computers to automatically repeat processes or instructions. This association has equivocally made us think that learning will be enhanced by the mere fact of acquiring computers or technological devices capable of reproducing the iterative process. Technological tools alone do not seem effective in enhancing the learning experience (McCabe and Meuter, 2011). Technology and pedagogy need to be well engrained for interactivity to yield a learning effect.

Moreover, it is important to take into account the existence of different types of interactivity that span from a single user interaction to more complex types of interactivity. The former just convey a reaction to a particular input (Sims 1997; 2003) often described in the literature. The latter can produce a particular cognitive effect in the user and are not commonly mentioned in academic papers for the novice of the research. Navigating by using interactivity in the context of a lesson is a natural type of single user interactivity to control the flow. Using ISAQ is a good example of a more complex type of interactivity. This book addressed this particular complexity and examined them in three different contexts.

Effective use of technology will require a paradigm shift from "teaching" to "learning" (Rogers, 2000) which will incorporate sound research on interactivity embedded with pedagogical strategies to enhance the learning experience. The research on "the effects of interactivity in e-learning system" contributes to reducing this vacuum of scientific evidence (Sims, 2003; Leiner and Quiring, 2008) and study interactivity within three main agents of the educational triangle: the learner, the teacher and the system.

The empirical studies related to each area of the educational triangle report significant results about the effects of interactivity in enhancing the learning experience. These results clearly show evidence of learning, on time, speeding and communicational effects caused by the use of interactivity in these contexts.

7.1 Interactivity in Pedagogical Feedback

The first empirical study (Chapter Four: Interactive Pedagogical Feedback) focused on Pedagogical feedback in the form of ISAQ that was incorporated in an academic lesson to determine the impact that different levels of interactivity have on students' memory and understanding. The ISAQ constitute an important feature of the two e-learning prototypes developed and their use allows students to evaluate their grasp of the material since immediate constructive feedback offers a valuable contribution to the learning experience.

The ISAQ' repeat functions may help to reduce the cognitive load generated by the intrinsic complexity of the lesson presented (Sweller & Chandler, 1994). Mental schemata (see section 2.3) require complex processes to organise information into meaningful cognitive containers in the individual mind. This information presents a degree of complexity that is directly dependent on the learner's previous knowledge. In other words, schemata in the mind of a mathematician are different to the schemata of the musician. Each expert has a particular mental map that will almost instantaneously make him able to recognise complex pattern related to his own area of expertise. When learner previous knowledge is high, his/her ability increases to assimilate new information related to this previous knowledge. On the contrary, if this knowledge is poor, however, the ISAQ interactive elements allow learners to rehearse almost instantaneously and validate their answers. It thus helps to create the appropriate individual schemata generating a learning effect. They are consistent with the theory of multimedia learning (Mayer, 1997) because meaningful learning takes place when relevant information in the ISAQ makes connections with corresponding representations in the individual cognition.

The ISAQ have a beneficial impact in student learning performance because they are able to construct their own understanding of the material. The potential for ISAQ implementation and fostering students' understanding is enormous: in both experiments implemented it has been observed to have a learning effect as a direct consequence of embedding interactivity in the e-learning systems.

They indicate in detail that the two groups with ISAQ (retention and transfer conditions) got a better performance than the control group in terms of overall scores. But when the two groups embedded with the ISAQ are compared, the group with the retention condition performs better than the group with the transfer condition in experiment #1, and the group with the transfer condition performs better in experiment #2. So in experiment #1 the results gave an indication that the ISAQ actually increase memory, and in experiment #2 the results gave an indication that the use of ISAQ promotes deep learning.

These results may be explained by the differences in LCMS that were used to deliver the lesson. The e-learning systems in experiment #1 used to deliver the lesson were developed in Adobe Authorware 7. It generated a stand-alone application that each student uses to learn the lesson. In experiment #2, the delivery mechanism was a web-based LCMS. Students accessed the educational material directly from the web server that hosted the learning objects that comprise the lesson. These differences in design allow the students in experiment #2 to acquire the material more quickly. The reflection time was thus greater, so may have had a greater cognitive impact. However, these ideas need to be investigated further to provide scientific evidence.

The initial experiment that was implemented using Authorware took longer to load the images and simulations required to present the content because of the design of the application. It was a stand-alone application designed to simultaneously load the flash and educational material. The flow of the lesson was therefore slower at the beginning. Students reported this static behaviour as inefficient, and it was corrected in the second experiment by using a different delivery mechanism. This behaviour introduced an extraneous cognitive load (Sweller & Chandler, 1994) that distracted the learner (see section 2.6.3).

Nevertheless, the results suggest that educational designers, who seek to foster learning, should incorporate interactive transfer questions in all their e-learning systems.

In the context of the experiment, the use of ISAQ clearly emphasizes the importance of the learning effect obtained by using interactivity. The ISAQ provide reflections on the new material and allow the amalgamation of the new and the existing knowledge by providing constructive feedback.

7.2 Interactivity in Audio Feedback

The second empirical study (Chapter Five: Interactive Audio Feedback) relates to the use of audio to enhance teacher capabilities to produce effective and quicker interactive feedback. Because for most people speaking is a much quicker form of communication than typing, the speed enhancements of speaking rather than typing are expected to be carried over to the process of creating feedback to enhance learning-related activities.

The study involved determining whether the speed enhancements of speaking rather than typing are carried over to the process of creating feedback. The investigation therefore sought to test the hypothesis that creating feedback in audio form is quicker than creating feedback in typewritten form. The investigation also analysed whether the phonetic benefits of audio over typewritten feedback are carried over to the learner. The study thus also sought to test the hypothesis that feedback received in audio form is better quality than feedback received in written form. Several experiments were designed to test these hypotheses under slightly different conditions. The results suggest that audio recording can decrease the time it takes to create feedback by 40-63 per cent. There are significant differences in the production of audio versus written feedback.

The availability of pen and paper in contrast to technological devices is controversial, and not related to the study. However, it will be interesting to evaluate the production of feedback using literally writing feedback (pen and paper) and compare the results to interactive audio feedback to determine the quicker method. In this study, writing feedback is synonymous with typing feedback since a computer and word processor are used to produce it. This technological contrast can be seen in the work of Sweller and Chandler (1994), who compare teaching CAD/CAM systems with a computer, or using other educational materials such as illustrations. They conclude that employing technological devices doesn't always speed up teaching or lead to better understanding.

In addition, there is an additional decrease of time with the introduction of the guiding template in experiment #4 (Figure 34 and Figure 35) that direct the procedure of taking notes when evaluating the presentations. According to the tutors, the guiding template helps to create a mental structure to follow while developing the audio feedback to keep consistency when developing all of the audio feedback. Lecturer attention is held by this template, which signals that the structure that should be consistent when producing the audio feedback. Behaviour is related to the signalling principle (see section 2.6.3) that recommends hints and cues in the organisation of a presentation (Mayer, 2005). It is also related to the multimedia principle of coherence (Moreno & Mayer, 1999) and the cognitive theory of multimedia learning (Mayer, 2005) since the template and the mental structure help to keep attention and the sequence required for developing the audio feedback.

Tutors reported that there was significant time saving in the process of creating the feedback. All tutors who were producing feedback preferred recording audio feedback because speaking is a more "natural" and effortless process than typing.

The use of interactive technology to create the audio feedback creates a kind of "speeding effect" in the production of the audio file. The effect was persistent across all the experiments. The creation of audio feedback can offer significant time savings to tutors compared with typed text. Modern developments in recording and delivering audio mean that providing audio feedback is now a real possibility for tutors. Not only does it appear to reduce the time taken for them to record the feedback, but it also appears to be a more natural and liberating process.

Although based on the results we can conclude that the production of interactive audio feedback is a more efficient method, it is important to evaluate whether content quality doesn't deteriorate during the process. Students' opinions validate that it doesn't deteriorate, but on the contrary is improved because of the added gains introduced by phonetics and personalisation. From the learners' perspective, audio feedback is richer and more authentic than written feedback. It appears to personalize the feedback relationship between tutor and learner, reducing the social space that often divides them. The use of interactivity creates a communicational effect because the students perceived that they received a more complete message when they listened the voice of the lecturer. This is consistent with the voice principle (see section 2.6.3) that recommends it is better if words are spoken in a standard accent by a human (Mayer, 2005). The human voice triggers a social response in the learner that encourages them to make sense of the information presented. It also added a personalised connotation to the feedback.

The experiments were developed following the nature cycle of the action research approach (Figure 5). After a sequential evaluation of each experiment (action evaluation), the results trigger a reflection and planning (action planning) work for the next phase to follow (action taking). The reflections on the pros and cons of the approach were taking into consideration when designing and implementing the subsequent experiment.

7.3 Interactivity in Texting Feedback

The latter study focused on the system that mediates the relation between the two main agents of the educational triangle: the teacher and the learner. The empirical study used texting messages (SMS) supported by a web-based response system to provide formative feedback to a student audience after educational content has been delivered. The system's feedback employed to communicate with teachers and learners is an easy to set up mechanism to integrate technology with pedagogical practices and learning activities.

The object of this experiment was to determine whether Interactive Texting Feedback is a valid and effective pedagogical approach to enhancing the learning experience. Inferential analysis demonstrates good correlations among the variables analysed that indicates that a learning effect has taken place.

The use of immediate interactive feedback as part of the particular technological setting in this research is innovative. It involves a large audience that contributes to validating the collective understanding of the lesson. The immediate feedback helps students to create concrete mental associations (schemata) between their prior experience (stored in LTM) and the new information taught (Wittrock 2010; 1974).

Significant results indicate that students consider this approach to be a viable contribution to learning, and it should spread to other modules in Brunel University. This is a cost-effective approach to learning since it is a new educational strategy where the students receive immediate constructive feedback and it motivates them to react in real time to the lesson presented.

Some considerations made regarding students' willingness to contribute with their messages (SMS) are important because it raises some ethical issues. However, given the nature and cost-effectiveness of the approach, it is recommended that they are managed by the administrators of the academic institution. It can provide some kind of reward or compensation.

7.4 Limitations of this Research

There are several limitations of this research that should be taken into consideration.

First, the Interactive Pedagogical Feedback study used only a limited number of ISAQ for each of the conditions (memory and transfer), because the main objective was to determine the existence of a learning effect. The addition of more ISAQ could show a different degree of the learning effect observed.

Second, the pedagogical design implemented is related to the heart and circulatory systems. Different subjects will require specific pedagogical designs. There is therefore a limitation in using only one subject. The effect of interactivity may be affected to a greater or lesser degree by the introduction of different pedagogy. However, it needs to be investigated.

Third, ethical considerations were taken into account to avoid the application of an innovative way of learning to only a particular part of the sample. This limited the ability to implement a pure experimental design.

Fourth, the level of actual interactivity manipulated in this study was useful at the time the study was conducted. Future research may be needed to revise other types of interactive elements incorporated in a lesson.

Fifth, the primary research was limited to Brunel University. Industry and other academic sectors interested in the research have to take this limitation into account. It could be useful to see the relationship between different institutions.

Sixth, the size of the sample may be considered a limitation, since the size of the example was approximately 30 students. Hence, it is possible that some selected samples may not be the most appropriate representatives for this study. However, statistically speaking, the use of t-test and other tools allow us to validate the results.

Seventh, the only reported downside of audio feedback (from the students' perspective) was that it was more difficult to navigate and focus on particular aspects of the narrative. However most believed this was more than compensated for by the richness of audio feedback.

Eighth, the contribution made by the interviewees influence the quality of the research conducted. In order to get honest and precise responses, the process was managed carefully. Lack of experience by the interviewer can affect the results. However the questions in all the interviews were designed to be straightforward and avoid little intervention of the interviewer. Future studies need to interview as many staff and students as possible.

Ninth, time was limited in the students interviewed because of the high demand placed on students by the activities. Participating in an interview was thus not a priority, leading them to rush the interviews, and giving some short answers

7.5 Conclusion

Significant differences were found in all the experiments that demonstrate that interactivity used in different contexts produced conclusive effects that enhance the learning experience in all the scenarios investigated (the educational triangle). The implications of using interactivity in any academic context, but specifically in Higher Education where these studies were conducted, are quite important. The students may have a better understanding of the lessons if ISAQ are incorporated into their academic content (Chapter Four Interactive Pedagogical Feedback).

Lecturers will reduce the time that it actually takes to produce feedback for students' submitted work. At the same time, students' comprehension of the feedback received will increase due to the paralinguistic features of the audio file recorded(Chapter Five Interactive Audio Feedback).

In addition, any classroom or academic room can be transformed into a high-tech ARS by inviting students to send SMS texts to a web portal using their mobile phones. The added advantage to this approach is the low cost of implementing it. (Chapter Six Interactive Texting Feedback).

In conclusion, a learning effect was recognized among all empirical studies, to a greater or lesser degree. It was first observed when pedagogical feedback in the form of ISAQ was incorporated in an academic lesson to determine the impact that different levels of interactivity have on students' memory and understanding. A learning effect was also reported on the reception of personalised audio feedback. Lecturers and learners using the texting feedback approach also noticed that comprehension of the material taught was improved. It enables lecturers to perceive immediately whether the learning message was delivered as intended. It is considered that interactivity used in the context of this research has the ability to help connectivity between new information and existing knowledge stored in LTM. It is thus easily retrievable. The ISAQ helps to create the appropriate individual schemata generating a learning effect. Meaningful learning takes place when relevant information in the ISAQ makes connections with corresponding representations in the individual cognition (LTM) according to the generative theory of learning (Wittrock, 2010; 1974)

The evidence of these findings contributes to supporting the long debate about the lack of demonstration to corroborate the effectiveness of interactivity in e-learning systems. The results provide tangible evidence of the interactivity effects. Moreover, they will serve as guidelines for instructional designers to maximise students' learning by using the appropriate type of interactivity related to the specific activity.

Furthermore, the results indicate that some types of interactivity produce the effect of increasing the learner's cognitive ability to remember information (memory effect), while other types of interactivity increase the learner's cognitive ability to understand the learning message (transfer effect). Adding interactivity of the two types will magnify the effects because it will increase memory and deep learning.

Feedback plays a fundamental role in the learning process, providing diagnosis and remedial suggestions for changing future actions (Kumar & Stracke, 2011; Wang & Wu, 2008). However, the timing of feedback given is vital. Poor timing indicates that the potential benefits of feedback are often not attained (Chanock, 2000; Duncan, 2007; Hounsell et al., 2008). Embedding Interactivity in feedback mechanisms has proved effective in the production and delivering of feedback to learners in e-learning systems.

7.6 Future Recommendations

Several recommendations have been already identified in the discussion of the findings. They are summarised, and the main recommendations are presented in the following paragraphs.

Implementation of the ISAQ within other educational subjects is recommended, but taking into consideration the pedagogical design inherent in each topic. For example, there is a difference in the approach to teaching mathematics and music. However, the constructive feedback within each ISAQ must be related to the lesson and should be part of the distracters. The difference between the correct answer and the distracters should therefore be recognized by knowledge acquired when learning the lesson.

Future research will incorporate a set of retention ISAQ combined into one system with another set of transfer ISAQ. Retention questions will create a basic knowledge that supports the deeper knowledge reinforced by the transfer ISAQ.

Interactivity performance was determined by results that evaluated short-term memories (Engle et al., 1999). The post-tests implemented were taken immediately after the conditions were applied. Assessments taken after a week, and a longer period of time, are recommended because they can provide information about how long learning lasts compared with relevant literature. Knowledge acquisition, and how long the information remains in memory (STM), and how it is degrading with time are important factors to be studied. An additional post-test could be applied at a later time to determine how long the information learned from the lesson lasts.

Another recommendation is related to the quantity of material in the lesson, and the number of ISAQ questions: although they are adequate for the purpose of this particular experiment, the length of the lesson and the number of questions could be increased for getting a broader perspective on the phenomena.

REFERENCES

Adair, J., & Vohra, N. (2003). The explosion of knowledge, references, and citations: Psychology's unique response to a crisis. *American Psychologist, 58(Jan)*(1), 15-23.

Altrichter, H., & Gstettner, P. (1993). Action research: A closed chapter in the history of german social science. *Education through Research, 1*(3), 329-60.

Anderson, J. R. (1982). Acquisition of cognitive skill. *Psychological Review, 89*(4), 369-406. doi:10.1037/0033-295X.89.4.369

—. (1993). Problem solving and learning. *American Psychologist, 48*(1), 35-44. doi:10.1037/0003-066X.48.1.35

Anderson, R. C., & Pearson, D. (2002). A schema-theoretic view of basic processes in reading comprehension. In M. L. Kamil (Ed.), *Methods of literacy research: The methodology chapters from the handbook of reading research* (volume 3 ed., pp. 255) L. Erlbaum Associates.

Angelo, T. A., & Cross, K. P. (1993). *Classroom assessment techniques: A handbook for college teachers.* San Francisco: Jossey-Bass.

Anson, C. M. (1999). Distant voices: Teaching and writing in a culture of technology. *College English, 61*(3), 261-280.

Antao, B. A. A., Brodersen, A. J., Bourne, J. R., & Cantwell, J. R. (1992). Building intelligent tutorial systems for teaching simulation in engineering education. *Education, IEEE Transactions on, 35*(1), 50-56.

Antâon, P. S., Silberglitt, R. S., Schneider, J., & Ebrary, I. (2001). *The global technology revolution : Bio/nano/materials trends and their synergies with information technology by 2015.* Santa Monica, CA: RAND. Retrieved from /z-wcorg/

Area, M. (2002). Integrating internet in adult education schools: The RedVEDA project. *Educational Technology & Society, 5*(1), 168.

Atkinson, R. C., & Shiffrin, R. M. (1968). Human memory: A proposed system and its control processes. In K. W. Spence, & J. T. Spence (Eds.), *The psychology of learning and motivation (vol. 2)* (pp. 89-195). New York: Academic Press.

Baddeley, A. D. (1986). *Working memory.* New York: Clarendon.

—. (1992). Working memory. *Science, 255*, 556-559.

Baddeley, A. D., & Hitch, G. J. (1974). Working memory. In G. A. Bower (Ed.), *Recent advances in learning and motivation (vol 8)* (pp. 47-90). New York: Academic Press.

Bandura, A. (1977). *Social learning theory*. Oxford England: Prentice-Hall.

—. (1986). *Social foundations of thought and action: A social cognitive theory* Englewood Cliffs, N.J. : Prentice-Hall.

Banks, D. A. (2009). Using audience response systems in the classroom. In David Banks (Ed.), *Encyclopedia of information science and technology, second edition* (pp. 3947-3952). US; Hershey, PA: IGI Global. doi:10.4018/978-1-60566-026-4.ch629

Bates, A. W., & Gary, P. (2003). *Effective teaching with technology in higher education*. San Francisco: Jossey-Bass Publishers.

Beatty, I., & Gerace, W. (2009). Technology-enhanced formative assessment: A research-based pedagogy for teaching science with classroom response technology. *Journal of Science Education and Technology, 18*(2), 146-162. doi:10.1007/s10956-008-9140-4

Beauchamp, G., & Kennewell, S. (2010). Interactivity in the classroom and its impact on learning. *Computers & Education, 54*(3), 759-766. doi:DOI: 10.1016/j.compedu.2009.09.033

Bell, B., & Cowie, B. (2001). The characteristics of formative assessment in science education. *Science Education, 85*(5), 536-553. doi:10.1002/sce.1022

Bell, M. (2007). In Mason (Ed.), *Managing diversity in organizations*. OH, USA: Thomson South-Western.

Bell, T., Cockburn, A., Wingkvist, A., & Green, R. (2007). Podcasts as a supplement in tertiary education: : An experiment with two computer science courses. In () Mobil Learning Technologies and Applications (MoLTA) 2007 Institute of Information and Mathematical Sciences, Massey University, Auckland, New Zealand.

Bergtrom, G. (2006). Clicker sets as learning objects. *Interdisciplinary Journal of Knowledge and Learning Objects, 2*, 02/02/2011.

Berk, L., & Winsler, A. (1995). Vygotsky's approach to development. In *In scaffolding children's learning: Vygotsky and early childhood learning* (pp. 25-34). Washington: Natl. Assoc for Educ. Of Young Children.

Biesta, G. J., & Burbules, N. C. (2003). *Pragmatism and educational research. lanham, MD: Rowman and littlefield.* Lanham, MD: Rowman and Littlefield.

Bitterman, M. E. (2006). Classical conditioning since pavlov. *Review of General Psychology, 10*(4), 365-376. doi:10.1037/1089-2680.10.4.365

Black, P., & Wiliam, D. (1998). Assessment and classroom learning. *Assessment in Education, 5*, 7-74.

Boud, D. (1995). *Enhancing learning through self-assessment.* London: Routledge.

Bourne, D. (1990). Computer-assisted instruction, learning theory, and hypermedia: An associative linkage. *Research Strategies, 8*(4), 160.

Bransford, J. D., Brown, A., & Cocking, R. (2000). *How people learn: Mind, brain, experience and school* (Expanded Edition ed.). Washington, DC: National Academy Press.

Brewer, J., & Hunter, A. (1989). *Multimethod research: A synthesis of styles*. Thousand Oaks, CA, US: Sage Publications, Inc.

Brown, S., & Knight, P. (1994). *Assessing learners in higher education.* London: Kogan Page.

Buchanan, T. (2000). The efficacy of a world-wide web mediated formative assessment. *Journal of Computer Assisted Learning, 16*, 193-200.

Carchiolo, V., Longheu, A., Malgeri, M., & Mangioni, G. (2007). A model for a web-based learning system. *Information Systems Frontiers, 9*(2), 267-282. doi:10.1007/s10796-006-9014-3

Card, S. K. T., Moran, P., & Newell, A. (1983). *The psychology of Human–computer interaction* (1st ed.). London: Lawrence Erlbaum Associates.

Carswell, L., Thomas, P., Petre, M., Price, B., & Richards, M. (2000). Distance education via the internet: The student experience. *British Journal of Educational Technology, 31*(1), 29-46. doi:10.1111/1467-8535.00133

Chan, T., Roschelle, J., His, S., Kinshuk, K., Sharples, M., Brown, T., et al. (2006). One-to-one technology-enhanced learning: An opportunity for global research. *Research and Practice in Technology Enhanced Learning, 1*(1), 3-29.

Chandler, P., & Sweller, J. (1991). Cognitive load theory and the format of instruction. *Cognition & Instruction, 8*(4), 293(40).

Chandler, P., & Sweller, J. (1996). Cognitive load while learning to use a computer program. *Applied Cognitive Psychology, 10*(2), 151(20).

Chandler, P., & Sweller, J. (1992). The split-attention effect as a factor in the design of instruction. *British Journal of Educational Psychology, 62*(2), 233-246.

Chanock, K. (2000). Comments on essays: Do students understand what tutors write? *Teaching in Higher Education, 5*(1), 95-106.

Chase, P. N. (1985). Designing courseware: Prompts from behavioral instruction. *The Behavior Analyst, 8*(1), 65-76.

Chinn, M. D., & Fairlie, R. W. (2010). ICT use in the developing world: An analysis of differences in computer and internet penetration. *Review of International Economics, 18*(1), 153-167. doi:10.1111/j.1467-9396.2009.00861.x

Chou, C. (2003). *Interactivity and interactive functions in web-based learning systems: A technical framework for designers* Blackwell Publishing Ltd. doi:10.1111/1467-8535.00326

Clark, R. C. (Ed.). (2001). *Learning from media* (ed ed.). Greenwich, CT: Information Age Publishing.

Clark, R. C., & Mayer, R. E. (2003). *E-learning and the science of instruction*. San Francisco: Jossey-Bass.

Clark, R.E. (Winter 1983) "Reconsidering Research on Learning from Media", *Review of Educational Research,* vol. 53, no. 4, pp. 445-459.

—. (2004). The classical origins of Pavlov's conditioning. *Integrative Psychological and Behavioral Science, 39*(4), 279-294. doi:10.1007/BF02734167

Cleland, A. A., & Pickering, M. J. (2006). Do writing and speaking employ the same syntactic representations? *Journal of Memory and Language, 54*(2), 185-198. doi:10.1016/j.jml.2005.10.003

Coghlan, D., & Brannick, T. (2001). *Doing action research in your own organization.* London: Sage publications.

Cohen, L., Manion, L., & Morrison, K. (2000). *Research methods in education* (5th ed.). London: Routledge Falmer.

Collins. (2000). *Collins english dictionary* (5th Edition ed.) Harper Collins Publishers.

Collins, L. J. (2006). Livening up the classroom -- using audience response systems to promote active learning. *Medical Reference Services Quarterly, 26*(1), 81.

Conole, G., Dyke, M., Oliver, M., & Seale, J. (2004). Mapping pedagogy and tools for effective learning design. *Computers & Education, 43*, 17-33.

Conole, G., & Oliver, M. (2002). Embedding theory into learning technology practice with toolkits. *Journal of Interactive Media in Education, 8*

Cooper, P. A. (1993). Paradigm shifts in designed instruction: From behaviourism to cognitivism to constructivism. *Educational Technology,, 33*(5), 12-19.

Cowan, N. (1995). *Attention and memory: An integrated framework.* New York: Oxford University Press.

—. (2001). The magical number 4 in short-term memory: A reconsideration of mental storage capacity. *Behavioral and Brain Sciences, 24*(01), 87. doi:null

Craik, F. I. M., & Lockhart, R. S. (1972). Levels of processing: A framework for memory research. *Journal of Verbal Learning and Verbal Behavior, 11*(6), 671-684. doi: 10.1016/S0022-5371(72)80001-X

Cumming, G. (1998). Artificial intelligence in education: An exploration. *Journal of Computer Assisted Learning, 14*(4), 251-259. doi:10.1046/j.1365-2729.1998.1440251.x

Denzin, N. K. (1978). The research act (2nd ed.). New York: McGraw-HI.

Dey, I. (2003). *Qualitative data analysis: A user friendly guide for social scientists* Routledge.

DfEE. (1998). *Initial teacher training national curriculum for the use of information and communications technology in subject teaching.* No. Circular 4/98 Annex B.). London: Department for Education and Employment.

—. (1999). *The national numeracy strategy.* London: DfEE.

Dobbs, M. F. (1996). Managing diversity: Lessons from the private sector. *Public Personnel Management, 25*, 351-368.

Doherty, R. W., & Hilberg, R. S. (2007). Standards for effective pedagogy, classroom organization, english proficiency, and student achievement. *Journal of Educational Research, 101*(1), 24-34.

Domagk, S., Schwartz, R. N., & Plass, J. L. (2010). Interactivity in multimedia learning: An integrated model. *Computers in Human Behavior, 26*(5), 1024-1033. doi:DOI: 10.1016/j.chb.2010.03.003

Dorman, T. (2008). Self-assessment in CPD: Lessons from the UK undergraduate and postgraduate education domains. *Journal of Continuing Education in the Health Professions, 28*(1), 32-37.

Douglas, D. E., & Van, D. V. (2004). Effectiveness of E-learning course materials for learning database management systems: An experimental investigation. *Journal of Computer Information Systems, 44*(4), 41-48.

Driscoll, M. (2000). *Psychology of learning for instruction* (2nd *ed.).* Needham Heights, MA: Allyn & Bacon.

Duffy, T. M., & Cunningham, D. J. (1996). Constructivism: Implications for the design and delivery of instruction. In D. H. Jonassen (Ed.), *Handbook of research for educational communications and technology* (1st ed., pp. 170-199). New York: Educational communications and technology : Simon & Schuster Macmillan.

Duncan, N. (2007). Feed-forward: Improving students' use of tutors' comments. *Assessment and Evaluation in Higher Education, 32*(3), 271-283.

Einstein, J., & Pollack, G. D. (2000). Why ad dollars are shifting to digital. *Brandweek, 41*(46), 30-33.

Ekstrom, J. J., Gorka, S., Kamali, R., Lawson, E., Lunt, B., Miller, J., & Reichgelt, H. (2006). The information technology model curriculum. *Journal of Information Technology Education, 5*

Eley, M. G. (1992). *Differential adoption of study approaches within individual students* Springer Netherlands. doi:10.1007/BF00145015

Engle, R. W., Tuholski, S. W., Laughlin, J. E., & Conway, A. R. A. (1999). Working memory, short-term memory, and general fluid intelligence: A latent-variable approach. *Journal of Experimental Psychology: General, 128*(3), 309-331. doi:10.1037/0096-3445.128.3.309

Entwistle, N. J., & Entwistle, A. (1991). *Contrasting forms of understanding for degree examinations: The student experience and its implications* Springer Netherlands. doi:10.1007/BF00132288

Evans, C. (2008). The effectiveness of m-learning in the form of podcast revision lectures in higher education. *Computers & Education, 50*(2), 491-498. doi:DOI: 10.1016/j.compedu.2007.09.016

Evans, C., & Gibbons, N. J. (2007). The interactivity effect in multimedia learning. *Computers & Education, 49*, 1147-1160.

Evans, C., & Palacios, L. A. (2010). Feedback on student assignments: Audio as an alternative to typing. Fifth Mediterranean Conference on Information Systems MCIS 2010 Proceedings, (28)

Evans, C., & Palacios, L. A. (2010). Using audio to enhance learner feedback. Paper presented at *the International Conference in Education and Management Technology (ICEMT), 2010 International Conference on,* Cairo, Egypt. 148-151. doi:10.1109/ICEMT.2010.5657683

Evans, C. & Palacios, L. A. (2011). Interactive feedback in the classroom using SMS messages. *IADIS International Conference IADIS e-Learning 2011*, Rome, Italy.

Evans, C., & Sabry, K. (2003). Evaluation of the interactivity of web-based learning systems: Principles and process. *Journal of Innovations in Education and Teaching International, 40*(1), 89-99.

Fantuzzo, J., & Atkins, M. (1992 Spring). Applied behavior analysis for educators: Teacher centered and classroom based. *Journal of Applied Behavior Analysis, 25*(1), 37-42. doi:10.1901/jaba.1992.25-37

Feinberg, S., & Murphy, M. (2000). Applying cognitive load theory to the design of web-based instruction. Paper presented at the *Professional Communication Conference, 2000. Proceedings of 2000 Joint IEEE International and 18th Annual Conference on Computer Documentation (IPCC/SIGDOC 2000),* 353-360.

Fies, C., & Marshall, J. (2006). Classroom response systems: A review of the literature. *Journal of Science Education and Technology, 15*(1), 101-109. doi:10.1007/s10956-006-0360-1

Fulford, C. P., & Zhang, S. (1993). Perceptions of interaction: The critical predictor in distance education. *American Journal of Distance Education, 7*(3), 8-21. doi:10.1080/08923649309526830

Furet, F., & Forster, E. (1981). *Interpreting the French revolution.* Cambridge; New York; Melbourne; Paris: Cambridge university press; Éditions de la Maison des sciences de l'homme. Retrieved from /z-wcorg/

Gagne, R. M. (1962). Military training and principles of learning. *American Psychologist, 17*(2), 83-91. doi:10.1037/h0048613

Gallimore, R., Goldenberg, C. N., & Weisner, T. S. (1993). The social construction and subjective reality of activity settings: Implications for community psychology. *American Journal of Community Psychology, 21*(4), 537-560. doi:10.1007/BF00942159

Garavan, H. (1998). Serial attention within working memory. *Memory & Cognition, 26*, 263-276.

Garnham, A. (2009). Cognitivism. *The Routledge Companion to Philosophy of Psychology.,* , 99.

Garzón, F. C., & Rodríguez, Á. G. (2009). Where is cognitive science heading? *Minds & Machines, 19*(3), 301(18).

Gauvain, M., & Cole, M. (1993). Interactions between learning and development. In *Readings on the development of children* (2nd ed., pp. 28). new york: w. h.freeman and company.

Geelan, D. R. (2001). The empty centre : Power/Knowledge, relationships and the myth of 'student centered teaching' in teacher education. *Australian Journal of Education, 26*(2)

Gibbs, G. (Ed.). (1999). *Using assessment strategically to change the way students learn* (S. Brown and A. Glasner (eds) ed.). uk: Open University Press.

Gibbs, G. (2003). Improving student learning through assessment. *Journal of Geography in Higher Education, 27*(2), 123-132. doi:10.1080/0309826032000107450

Gikandi, J. W., Morrow, D., & Davis, N. E. (2011). Online formative assessment in higher education: A review of the literature. *Computers & Education, 57*(4), 2333-2351. doi:10.1016/j.compedu.2011.06.004

Gill, J., & Johnson, P. (1997). *Research methods for manager*. London: Paul Chapman Publishing Ltd.

Gould, J. D. (1978). How experts dictate. human perception and performance. *Journal of Experimental Psychology, 4*(4), 648-661.

—. (1982). Writing and speaking letters and messages. *International Journal of Man-Machine Studies, 16*(2), 147-171. doi:10.1016/S0020-7373(82)80054-0

Grabowski, J. (2010). Speaking, writing, and memory span in children: Output modality affects cognitive performance. *International Journal of Psychology, 45(1)*(Nov), 28-39.

Guild, P. B. (1997). Where do the learning theories overlap? *Educational Leadership, 55*(1), 30.

Hakkarainen, K. (2009). Three generations of technology-enhanced learning. *British Journal of Educational Technology, 40*(5), 879-889. doi:10.1111/j.1467-8535.2008.00873.x

Halfpenny, P.(1982). *Positivism and sociology: Explaining social life*. London: George Allen & Unwin.

Hannafin, M. J. (1989). Interaction strategies and emerging instructional technologies: Psychological perspectives. *Canadian Journal of Educational Communication, 18*(3), 167-179.

Hannafin, M. J., Phillips, T., Rieber, L. P., & Garhart, C. (1987). The effects of orienting activities and cognitive processing time on factual and inferential learning. *Educational Communications and Technology Journal, 35*, 75-84.

Hannafin, M. J., Phillips, T., & Tripp, S. (1986). The effects of orienting, processing, and practicing activities on learning from interactive video. *Journal of Computer-Based Instruction, 13*, 134-139.

Hannafin, R., & Sullivan, H. (1995). *Learner control in full and lean CAI programs* Springer Boston. doi:10.1007/BF02300479

Hartley, J. R. (1985). Some psychological aspects of computer-assisted learning and teaching. *Programmed Learning and Educational Technology, 22*(2), 140-149.

Hartsell, T. (2006). *Learning theories and technology: Practical applications*. US: doi:10.4018/ijicte.2006010105

Heilesen, S. B. (2010). What is the academic efficacy of podcasting? *Computers & Education, 55*(3), 1063-1068.
doi:DOI: 10.1016/j.compedu.2010.05.002

Hennessy, S., Deaney, R., Ruthven, K., & Winterbottom, M. (2007). Pedagogical strategies for using the interactive whiteboard to foster learner participation in school science. *Learning, Media and Technology, 32*(3), 283.

Hill, C. (1984). *The world turned upside down: Radical ideas during the English revolution* Penguin Group.

Hofer, B. K., & Pintrich, P. R. (1997). The development of epistemological theories: Beliefs about knowledge and knowing and their relation to learning. *Review of Educational Research, 67*(1), 88-140. doi:10.3102/00346543067001088

Holmes, N., Robson, E. H., & Steward, A. P. (1985). *Learner control in computer-assisted learning** Blackwell Publishing Ltd. doi:10.1111/j.1365-2729.1985.tb00017.x

Honebein, P., Duffy, T. M., & Fishman, B. (1993). Constructivism and the design of learning environments: Context and authentic activities for learning. In T. Duffy, J. Lowyck & D. H. Jonassen (Eds.), *The design of constructivist learning environments: Implications for instructional design and the use of technology.* (). Heidelberg: Springer-Verlag.

Hounsell, D., McCune, V., Hounsell, J., & Litjens, J. (2008). The quality of guidance and feedback to students, *Higher Education Research and Development, 27*(1), 55-67.

Howard, J. R. (2002). Do college students participate more in discussion in traditional delivery courses or in interactive telecourses? a preliminary comparison. *The Journal of Higher Education, 73*(6), 764-780.

Jackson, M., Ganger, A. A., Bridge, P. D., & Ginsburg, K. (2005). Wireless handheld computers in the undergraduate medical curriculum. *Medical Education Online, 10*(5)

Jacobs, H. H. (1989). *Interdisciplinary curriculum: Design and implementation.* Alexandria, VA: Association for Supervision and Curriculum Development.

Jiang, J., Kohler, J., MacWilliams, C., Zaletelj, J., Guntner, G., Horstmann, H., et al. (2011). LIVE: An integrated production and feedback system for intelligent and interactive TV broadcasting. Broadcasting, IEEE Transactions on, 57(3), 646-661.

Jick, T. D. (1979). Mixing qualitative and quantitative methods: Triangulation in action. *Administrative Science Quarterly, 24*(4), 602-611.

Johnson, C. I., & Mayer, R. E. (2009). A testing effect with multimedia learning. *Journal of Educational Psychology, 101*(3), 621-629. doi:10.1037/a0015183

Johnson, R. B., & Onwuegbuzie, A. J. (2004). Mixed methods research: A research paradigm whose time has come. *Educational Researcher, 33*(7), 14-26. doi:10.3102/0013189X033007014

Jonassen, D. H. (1999). Designing constructivist learning environments. In C. Reigeluth (Ed.), *Instructional design theories and models: A new paradigm of instructional theory* (Vol. II ed., pp. 215-239). Mahwah, NJ: Lawrence Erlbaum Associates.

Jones, J., & McNaught, C. (2011). In Ferrer N. F., Alfonso J. M.(Eds.), *Learning object evaluation and reuse: A hong kong experience* Springer New York. doi:10.1007/978-1-4419-6959-0_9

Kahiigi, E. K., Ekenberg, L., Hansson, H., Tusubira, F. F., & Danielson, M. (2007). Exploring the e-Learning state of art. Paper presented at the *6th European Conference on e-Learning,* Copenhagen Business School, Denmark. Retrieved from /z-wcorg/ database.

Kartal, G. (2010). Does language matter in multimedia learning? personalization principle revisited. *Journal of Educational Psychology, 102*(3), 615-624. doi:10.1037/a0019345

Kay, R. H., & LeSage, A. (2009). Examining the benefits and challenges of using audience response systems: A review of the literature. *Computers & Education, 53*(3), 819-827. doi:DOI: 10.1016/j.compedu.2009.05.001

Kemmis, S., & McTaggart, R. (1998). *The action research planner* (2nd edition ed.). Geloong, Victoria,Australia: Deaking University press.

Kemp, P. K., Myers, C. E., Campbell, M. R., & Pratt, A. P. (2010). Student perceptions and the effectiveness of podcasting in an associate degree nursing program. *Teaching and Learning in Nursing, 5*(3), 111-114. doi:DOI: 10.1016/j.teln.2010.01.006

Khan, K. S., Davies, D. A., & Gupta, J. K. (2001). Formative self-assessment using multiple true-false questions on the internet: Feedback according to confidence about correct knowledge. *Medical Teacher, 23*, 158-163.

Kirsh, D. (1997). *Interactivity and multimedia interfaces* Springer Netherlands. doi:10.1023/A:1002915430871

Knight, S. (2007, Effective practice with e-Learning: A good practice guide in designing for learning. *Joint Information Systems Committee,*

Köhler, W. (1927). *The mentality of apes* (2nd ed.). New York: Harcourt, Brace & Co.

Kohno, T. (2004). Analysis of an electronic voting system. Paper presented at the 27.

Kuhn, T. S. (1962). *The structure of scientific revolutions* (3rd ed.). USA: University of Chicago Press.

Kumar, V., & Stracke, E. (2011). Examiners' reports on theses: Feedback or assessment? *Journal of English for Academic Purposes, 10*(4), 211-222. doi:10.1016/j.jeap.2011.06.00

Lai, T. L. (2004). Service quality and perceived value's impact on satisfaction, intention and usage of short message service (SMS). *Information Systems Frontiers, 6*(4), 353-368. doi:10.1023/B:ISFI.0000046377.32617.3d

Lamos, J. P. (1984). Programmed instruction to computer-based instruction: The evolution of an instructional technology. In r. k. Bass, & d. b. Lumsdem (Eds.), *Instructional development: The state of the art* (). OK:USA: Mcalesters.

Lang, M. (2006). Hypermedia and associated concepts. In M. Lang (Ed.), *Encyclopedia of E-commerce, E-government, and mobile commerce* (pp. 565-572). US; Hershey, PA: IGI Global. doi:10.4018/978-1-59140-799-7.ch091

Lau, R. Y. K., Ip, R. K. F., Chan, M. T., Kwok, R. C. -., Wong, S. W. M., So, J. C. F., & Wong, E. Y. W. (2010). Podcasting: An internet-based social technology for blended learning. *Internet Computing, IEEE, 14*(3), 33-41.

Lawless, K. A., & Brown, S. W. (1997). *Multimedia learning environments: Issues of learner control and navigation* Springer Netherlands. doi:10.1023/A:1002919531780

Leonard, D. C. (2002). *Learning theories, A to Z.* Westport, Conn.: Oryx Press.

Levy, P., Ford, N., Foster, J., Madden, A., Miller, D., Nunes, M. B., . . . Webber, S. (2003). Educational informatics: An emerging research agenda. *Journal of Information Sytem, Pp, 29*(4), 298-310.

Leiner, D.J. and Quiring, O. (2008) "What Interactivity Means to the User Essential Insights into and a Scale for Perceived Interactivity", *Journal of Computer-Mediated Communication,* vol. 14, no. 1, pp. 127-155

Lewis, R. (1986). What is open learning? *Open Learning: The Journal of Open, Distance and e-Learning, 1*(2), 5-10. doi:10.1080/0268051860010202

Lim, C. (2004). *Engaging learners in online learning environments* Springer Boston. doi:10.1007/BF02763440

Lindquist, E. F. (1940). *Statistical analysis in educational research* Houghton Mifflin Boston.

Lindsay, E., & Good, M. (2009). The impact of audiovisual feedback on the learning outcomes of a remote and virtual laboratory class. *IEEE Transactions on Education, 52*(4), 491-502. doi:10.1109/TE.2008.930510

Lipponen, L. (2002). Exploring foundations for computer-supported collaborative learning. *Proceedings of the Conference on Computer Support for Collaborative Learning: Foundations for a CSCL Community,* Boulder, Colorado. 72-81.

Lu, H., & Chiou, M. (2010). The impact of individual differences on e-Learning system satisfaction: A contingency approach. *British Journal of Educational Technology, 41*(2), 307-323. doi:10.1111/j.1467-8535.2009.00937.x

Lunts, E. (2002). What does the literature say about the effectiveness of learner control in computer-assisted instruction? *Electronic Journal for the Integration of Technology in Education, 1*(2)

Luria, A. (Ed.). (1973). *The working brain: An introduction to neuropsychology*. New York: Basic Books.

McCabe, D. B., & Meuter, M. L. (2011). A student view of technology in the classroom. *Journal of Marketing Education, 33*(2), 149-159. doi:10.1177/0273475311410847

Mann, S. J. (2001). Alternative perspectives on the student experience: Alienation and engagement. *Studies in Higher Education, 26*(1), 7-19. doi:10.1080/03075070020030689

Manogue, M., Kelly, M., Masaryk, S. B., Brown, G., Catalanotto, F., Delap, E., Morio, I. (2002). Evolving methods of assessment. *European Journal of Dental Education, 6*, 53-66.

Manouselis, N., Drachsler, H., Vuorikari, R., Hummel, H., & Koper, R. (2011). Recommender systems in technology enhanced learning. In F. Ricci, L. Rokach, B. Shapira & P. B. Kantor (Eds.), *Recommender systems handbook* (pp. 387-415) Springer US. doi:10.1007/978-0-387-85820-3_12

Markett, C., Arnedillo, S. I., Weber, S., & Tangney, B. (2004). Pls turn ur mobile on: Short message service (SMS) supporting interactivity in the classroom. *Cognition and Exploratory Learning in Digital Age,* Lisbon. 475-478.

Markett, C., Arnedillo, S. I., Weber, S., & Tangney, B. (2004). Pls turn ur mobile on: Short message service (SMS) supporting interactivity in the classroom. *Cognition and Exploratory Learning in Digital Age,* Lisbon. 475-478.

Markett, C., Sánchez, I. A., Weber, S., & Tangney, B. (2006). Using short message service to encourage interactivity in the classroom. *Computers & Education, 46*(3), 280-293. doi:DOI: 10.1016/j.compedu.2005.11.014

Mayer, R. E. (1997). Multimedia learning: Are we asking the right questions? *Educational Psychologist, 32*, 1-19.

—. (2001). *Multimedia learning*. New York: Cambridge University Press.

—. (2003). Elements of a science of e-Learning. *Journal Educational Computing Research, 29*(3), 297-313.

—. (2005). *The Cambridge handbook of multimedia learning*. uk: Cambridge University Press.

Mayer, R. E., & Anderson, R. B. (1992). The instructive animation: Helping students build connections between words and pictures in multimedia learning. *Journal of Educational Psychology, 84*, 444-452.

Mayer, R. E., & Chandler, P. (2001). When learning is just a click away: Does simple user interaction foster deeper understanding of multimedia messages. *Journal of Educational Psychology, 93*, 390-397.

Mayer, R. E., Dow, G. T., & Mayer, S. (2003). Multimedia learning in an interactive self-explaining environment: What works in the design of agent-based microworlds? *Journal of Educational Psychology, 95*(4), 806-812. doi:10.1037/0022-0663.95.4.806

Mayer, R. E., & Gallini, J. K. (1990). When is an illustration worth ten thousand words? *Journal of Educational Psychology, 82*, 715-726.

Mayer, R. E., & Moreno, R. (1998). A cognitive theory of multimedia learning: Implications for design principles.

Mayer, R. E., & Moreno, R. (1998). A split-attention effect in multimedia learning: Evidence for dual processing systems in working.. *Journal of Educational Psychology, 90*(2), 312(9).

Mayer, R. E., Moreno, R., Boire, M., & Vagge, S. (1999). Maximizing constructivist learning from multimedia communications by minimizing cognitive load. *Journal of Educational Psychology, 91*(4), 638-643. doi:10.1037/0022-0663.91.4.638

Maxwell, J. A., & Miller, B. A. (2008). Categorizing and connecting strategies in qualitative data analysis. *Handbook of Emergent Methods*, 461-477.

McIntosh, N. (1996). Why do we lecture? *ReproLine ®The Reading Room.*, (JHPIEGO Strategy Paper), 01feb,2011.

McKimm, J. (2003). Assuring quality and standards in teaching. In H. Fry, S. Ketteridge & S. Marshall (Eds.), *Handbook for teaching and learning in higher education* (2nd edition ed.,). london ,UK: kogan page.

McPherson, M., & Nunes, M. B. (2004). *Developing innovation in online learning: An action research framework* (1st ed.). London: Routledge Falmer.

Megzari, O., Yuan, L., & Karmouch, A. (2002). *Meta-data and media management in a multimedia interactive telelearning system* Springer Netherlands. doi:10.1023/A:1013297803500

Miller, E. (1999). Positivism and clinical psychology. *Clinical Psychology & Psychotherapy, 6*(1), 1-6. doi:10.1002/(SICI)1099-0879(199902) 6:1<1::AID-CPP180>3.0.CO;2-R

Miller, G. A. (1956). The magical number seven, plus or minus two: Some limits on our capacity for processing information. *Psychological Review, 63*, 81-97.

Moore, M. G. (1989). Editorial: Three types of interaction. *The American Journal of Distance Education, 3*, 1-6.

Morabito, J. I., Sack, I., & Bhate, A. (1999). *Organization modeling: Innovative architectures for the 21st century*. Upper Saddle River, NJ:Prentice Hall:

Moreno, R., & Mayer, R. E. (1999). Cognitive principles of multimedia learning: The role of modality and contiguity. *Journal of Educational Psychology, 91*(2), 358-368. doi:10.1037/0022-0663.91.2.358

Morss, K., & Murray, R. (2005). *Teaching at universities: A guide for postgraduates and researchers* Sage Publications.

Murphy, J. P. (1990). *Pragmatism: From peirce to davidson*. Boulder,CO: Westview.

Niaz, M. (2008). A rationale for mixed methods (integrative) research programmes in education. *Journal of Philosophy of Education, 42*(2), 287-305. doi:10.1111/j.1467-9752.2008.00625.x

Northedge, A. (2003). Rethinking teaching in the context of diversity. *Teaching in Higher Education, 8*(1)

Oberauer, K. (2002). Access to information in working memory: Exploring the focus of attention. *Journal of Experimental Psychology: Learning, Memory, and Cognition, 28*(3), 411-421. doi:10.1037/0278-7393.28.3.411

—. (2006). Is the focus of attention in working memory expanded through practice? *Journal of Experimental Psychology: Learning, Memory, and Cognition, 32*(2), 197-214. doi:10.1037/0278-7393.32.2.197

Olson, J. R. (1988). *Schoolwords/Microworlds: Computers and the culture of school*. Oxford: Pergamon.

Olson, J. R., & Olson, G. M. (1990). The growth of cognitive modeling in human-computer interaction since GOMS. *Human-Computer Interaction, 5*(2), 221.

Orey, M. A., & Nelson, W. A. (1991). Using intelligent tutoring design principles to integrate cognitive theory into computer-based instruction.

Ormrod, J. E. (2004). *Human learning* (fith ed.) Merrill.

Oxford Dictionaries. (2010). *"Evidence". oxford dictionaries.*

Oxford University Press USA. (2009). *Podcast" is the word of the year.*

Ozkan, S., & Koseler, R. (2009). Multi-dimensional students' evaluation of e-Learning systems in the higher education context: An empirical investigation. *Computers & Education, 53*(4), 1285-1296. doi:DOI: 10.1016/j.compedu.2009.06.011

Paivio, A. (1986). *Mental representations : A dual coding approach.* New York ; Oxford University Press ; Oxford: Clarendon.

Palacios, L. A. (2002). Innovative gateway to learning objects. Paper presented at the *International Conference for Information and Communication Technologies in Education,*

—. (2002). Learning objects and the GUARDIANS system. *Computer Assisted Learning Research Group, International Conference,*

—. (2005). Action research for developing learning objects in medical eCPD. *International Conference Sponsored by the European Association of Distance Teaching Universities (EADTU).* Rome, Italy.

—. (2008). Travel medicine online: The eCpd experience. Paper presented at the *Fifth Pan-Commonwealth Forum ,* 354.

Palacios, L. A., & Evans, C. (2010). Effectiveness of interactivity for enhanced undergraduate learning. In M. Siran, & T. Purnendu (Eds.), *Cases on transnational learning and technologically enabled Environments* (pp. 359-375) IGI Global. doi:10.4018/978-1-61520-749-7

Palacios, L. A., & Evans, C. (2010). Interactive self-assessment questions within a virtual environment, proc. third international. Paper presented at the *Conference on Innovations in Learning for the Future 2010: E-Learning,* Istanbul, Turkey, Istanbul Kültür University. (May 10-14)

Palacios, L. A., & Evans, C. (2011). Interactive self-assessment questions within a virtual Environment . *International Journal of E-Adoption (IJEA), 3*(2), 1-10. doi:10.4018/jea.2011040101

Pavlovs, I. P. (1906). The scientific investigation of the psychical faculties or processes in the higher animals. *Science, 24*(620), pp. 613-619.

Pfaffenberge, B. r., Schafer, S. M., White, C., & Karow, B. (Eds.). (2004). *HTML, XHTML, and CSS bible* (3rd ed.). Indianapolis: Wiley Publishing.

Pituch, K. A., & Lee, Y. (2006). The influence of system characteristics on e-Learning use. *Computers & Education, 47*(2), 222-244. doi:DOI: 10.1016/j.compedu.2004.10.007

Reeves, T. (2002). Storm clouds on the digital education horizon. *Proceedings of the 19th Annual Conference of the Australasian Society for Computers in Learning in Tertiary Education (ASCILITE 2002),* Aukckland, New Zealand. 17-26.

Requin, J., Stelmach, G. E., North Atlantic Treaty Organization. Scientific Affairs Division., & NATO Advanced Study Institute on Tutorials in Motor Neuroscience. (1991). *Tutorials in motor neuroscience.* Paper presented at the Retrieved from /z-wcorg/ database.

Rieber, L. P. (1990). Using computer animated graphics with science instruction with children. *Journal of Educational Psychology, 82*(1), 135-140. doi:10.1037/0022-0663.82.1.135

Riordan, B., & Traxler, J. (2005). The use of targeted bulk SMS texting to enhance student support, inclusion and retention. Paper presented at the *Wireless and Mobile Technologies in Education, 2005. WMTE 2005. IEEE International Workshop on,* 4 pp.

Robinson, M. (1979). *Classroom control: Some cybernetic comments on the possible and the impossible* Springer Netherlands. doi:10.1007/BF00117013

Rogers, D. L. (2000). A paradigm shift: Technology integration for higher education in the new millennium. *AACE Journal, 1*(13), 19-33.

Rojas-Drummond, S., & Mercer, N. (2003). Scaffolding the development of effective collaboration and learning. *International Journal of Educational Research, 39*(1-2), 99-111. doi:DOI: 10.1016/S0883-0355(03)00075-2

Rose, N. S., Myerson, J., Roediger, H. L. I.,II, & Hale, S. (2010). Similarities and differences between working memory and long-term memory: Evidence from the levels-of-processing span task. *Journal of Experimental Psychology: Learning, Memory, and Cognition, 36*(2), 471-483. doi:10.1037/a0018405

Rothkopf, E. Z. (1966). Learning from written instructive materials: An exploration of the control of inspection behavior by test-like events. *American Educational Research Journal, 3*(4), 241-249. doi:10.3102/00028312003004241

Rousseau, B., Browne, P., Malone, P., & Ó Foghlú, M. (2004). User profiling for content personalisation in information retrieval. *19th Annual Conf. of ACM Symposium on Applied Computing (ACMSAC04),* Nicosia, Cyprus.

Russell, T., & Munby, H. (1992). *Teachers and teaching: From classroom to reflection.* London: Falmer Press.

Salisbury, D. (1988). Effective drill and practice strategies. In *Instructional designs for microcomputer courseware* (D. Jonassen (Ed.) ed., pp. 103-124). NJ,Erlbaum: Hillsdale.

Schar, S. G., & Krueger, H. (2000). Using new learning technologies with multimedia. *IEEE Multimedia, 7*(3), 40-51.
Schwandt, T. A. (1994). Constructivist, interpretivist approaches to human inquiry. In N. K. Denzin, & Y. S. Lincoln (Eds.), *Handbook of qualitative research* (pp. 118-137) Thousand Oaks: Sage Publications.
Schrum, L., & Berge, Z. (1997). Creating student interaction within the educational experience: A challenge for online educators. *Canadian Journal of Educational Communication, 26*(3), 133-144.
Scornavacca, E., & Marshall, S. (2007). TXT-2-LRN: Improving students' learning exper ience in the classroom through interactive SMS. Paper presented at the *System Sciences, 2007. HICSS 2007. 40th Annual Hawaii International Conference on,* 5-5.
Seels, B., & Richey, R. (1994). *Instructional technology: The definition and domains of the field.* Washington, D.C.: Association for Educational Communications and Technology.
Sechrest, L., & Sidana, S. (1995). Quantitative and qualitative methods: Is there an alternative? *Evaluation and Program Planning, 18*, 77-87.
Shankar, T. R. (2006). Speaking on the record: A theory of composition. *Computers and Composition, 23*(3), 374-393. doi:10.1016/j.compcom.2006.05.002
Sharples, M., Taylor, J., & Vavoula, G. (2005). Towards a theory of mobile learning. *In Proceedings of mLearn 2005 Conference,* Cape Town, South Africa.
Shulman, L. S. (1986). Paradigms and research programs in the study of teaching: A contemporary perspective. In handbook of research in teaching (3rd ed.). New York: Macmillan: M.C. Witrock.
—. (1987). Knowledge and teaching: Foundations of the new reform. *Harvard Educational Review, 57*, 1-22.
Shute, V. J. (2008). Focus on formative feedback. *Review of Educational Research, 78*(1), 153-189. doi:10.3102/0034654307313795
Siau, K., Sheng, H., & Nah, F. (2006). Use of classroom response system to enhance classroom interactivity. *IEEE Transactions on Education, 49*(3), 398-403.
Siemens, G. (2004). Connectivism: A learning theory for the digital age. *International Journal of Instructional Technology and Distance Learning, 2.1*, 3-10.
—. (2006). *Connectivism: Learning theory or pastime of the self-amused?* Retrieved 03/07/, 2013, from http://www.elearnspace.org/Articles/connectivism_self-amused.htm
Singley, K., & Anderson, J. R. (1989). *The transfer of cognitive skill.* Cambridge, MA: Harvard University Press.

Sims, K. (1994). Evolving 3D morphology and behavior by competition. *Artificial Life IV Proceedings,* 28–39.

Sims, R.C. (2003) "Promises of Interactivity: Aligning Learner Perceptions and Expectations with Strategies for Flexible and Online Learning", *Distance Education,* vol. 24, no. 1, pp. 87

—. (1996). Engagement, control and the learner: A theoretical appraisal of interactivity. *Proceedings of the 13th Annual Conference of the Australian Society for Computers in Learning in Tertiary Education,* Adelaide, SA: University of South Australia.

—. (1997). Interactive learning as an "emerging" technology: A reassessment of interactive and instructional design strategies. *Australian Journal of Educational Technology, 13*(1), 68-84.

Sims, K. (1992). *Choreographed image flow* John Wiley & Sons, Ltd. doi:10.1002/vis.4340030106

Siran, M., & Purnendu, T. (2010). *Cases on transnational learning and technologically enabled Environments* [ ] IGI Global. doi:10.4018/978-1-61520-749-7

Skinner, B. F. (1953). *Science and human behavior.* New York: Macmillan.

—. (2009). About behaviourism In B. O. Miller (Ed.), *Foundations of psychological thought: A history of psychology.* (pp. 261-278). Thousand Oaks, CA US: Sage Publications, Inc.

Smits, M. H. S. B., Boon, J., Sluijsmans, D. M. A., & van Gog, T. (2008). Content and timing of feedback in a web-based learning environment: Effects on learning as a function of prior knowledge. *Interactive Learning Environments, 16*(2), 183-193. doi:10.1080/10494820701365952

Søndergaard, H., & Thomas, D. (2004). Effective feedback to small and large classes," , october . *34th ASEE/IEEE Frontiers in Education Conference,* 20 – 23.

Stergioulas, L. K., Minetou, C., Koskinen, T., Klein, M., Dang, J., Denual, Y., Makropoulos, K. (2004). Roadmap for the future of eTraining/ eLearning technologies in europe. Paper presented at the *Advanced Learning Technologies, 2004. Proceedings. IEEE International Conference on,* 460-464.

Stone, A., Briggs, J., & Smith, C. (2002). SMS and interactivity-some results from the field, and its implications on effective uses of mobile technologies in education. Paper presented at the *Wireless and Mobile Technologies in Education, 2002. Proceedings. IEEE International Workshop on,* 147-151.

Storck, J., & Sproull, L. (1995). Through a glass darkly what do people learn in videoconferences? *Human Communication Research, 22*(2), 197-219. doi:10.1111/j.1468-2958.1995.tb00366.x

Sundberg, P. (2003). *Concept map of learning theories.* Retrieved 2/9/2011, 2011, from http://www.ed.uiuc.edu/courses/edpsy317/sp03/learning-maps/sundberg-learning-theories.gif

Sweller, J. (1988). *Cognitive load during problem solving: Effects on learning* Lawrence Erlbaum Associates, Inc. doi:10.1207/s15516709cog1202_4

Sweller, J., & Chandler, P. (1991). Evidence for cognitive load theory. *Cognition & Instruction, 8*(4), 351(12).

Sweller, J., & Chandler, P. (1994). Why some material is difficult to learn. *Cognition & Instruction, 12*(3), pp185.

Sweller, J., Chandler, P., Tierney, P., & Cooper, M. (1990). Cognitive load as a factor in the structuring of technical material. *Journal of Experimental Psychology: General, 119*(2), 176-192. doi:10.1037/0096-3445.119.2.176

Tavangarian, D., Leypold, M. E., Nölting, K., Röser, M., & Voigt, D. (2004). Is e-Learning the solution for individual learning? *Electronic Journal of e-Learning, 2*(2), 273-280.

Tempelman-Kluit, N. (2006). Multimedia learning theories and online instruction. *College & Research Libraries, 67*(4), 364-369.

Tesch, R. (1990). *Qualitative research: Analysis types and software tools.* Bedford: LSL press.

The Quality Assurance Agency for Higher Education (QAA).*Programme specifications.* Retrieved 5/24/2011, 2011, from http://www.qaa.ac.uk/academicinfrastructure/programSpec/guidelines06.asp

Tinsley, R., & Lebak, K. (2009). Expanding the zone of reflective capacity: Taking separate journeys together. *Networks:Online Journal for Tearcher Research, 11*(2)

Tullock, G. (1971). The paradox of revolution. Public Choice, 11(1), 89-99. doi:10.1007/BF01726214

TurningPoint. (2007). Audience response system (clickers). *Journal of Technology in Human Services, 25*(3), 107.

Van Lier, L. (2000). From input to affordance: Social-interactive learning from an ecological perspective. In J. Lantolf (Ed.), *Sociocultural theory and second language learning* (pp. 245-261). New York: Oxford University Press.

Velan, G. M., Kumar, R. K., Dziegielewski, M., & Wakefield, D. (2002). Web-based self-assessments in pathology with questionmark perception. *Pathology, 34*, 282-284.

Verhaeghen, P., & Basak, C. (2005). Ageing and switching of the focus of attention in working memory: Results from a modified *N*-back task. *The Quarterly Journal of Experimental Psychology Section A: Human Experimental Psychology, 58*(1), 134.

Vygotsky, L. (1978). Interactions between learning and development. *Mind and Society,* , 79-91.

Wager, W., & Wager, S. (1985). Presenting questions, processing responses, and providing feedback in CAI. *Journal of Instructional Development, 8*(4), 2-8. doi:10.1007/BF02906047

Wang, M. J., & Shen, R. M. (2008). Increasing interactivity in large blended classrooms through a cutting-edge mobile learning system. Paper presented at the *Information & Communications Technology, 2008. ICICT 2008. ITI 6th International Conference on,* 59-63.

Wang, S., & Wu, P. (2008). The role of feedback and self-efficacy on web-based learning: The social cognitive perspective. *Computers & Education, 51*(4), 1589-1598. doi:10.1016/j.compedu.2008.03.004

Wang, T. H. (2007). What strategies are effective for formative assessment in an e-Learning environment? *Journal of Computer Assisted Learning, 23*(3), 171-186. doi:10.1111/j.1365-2729.2006.00211.x

Washburne, J. N. (1936). The definition of learning. *Journal of Educational Psychology, 27*(8), 603-611. doi:10.1037/h0060154

Watkins, R. (2010). e-Learning. In *Handbook of improving performance in the workplace: Selecting and implementing performance interventions* (pp. 577-597) John Wiley & Sons, Inc. doi:10.1002/9780470587102.ch24

Webler, T., Levine, D., Rakel, H., & Renn, O. (1991). A novel approach to reducing uncertainty: The group delphi. *Technological Forecasting and Social Change, 39*(3), 253-263. doi:DOI: 10.1016/0040-1625(91)90040-M

Webster, J., & Hackley, P. (1997). Teaching effectiveness in technology-mediated distance learning. *Academy of Management Journal, 40*(6), 1282-1309.

Wetzel, C. D., Radtke, P. H., & Stem, H. W. (1994). *Instructional effectiveness of video media*. NJ: Erlbaum: Hillsdale.

Wiersma, W., & Jurs, S. G. (2005). *Research methods in education* Allyn and Bacon.

Wilson, M. (1999). Student-generated multimedia presentations: Tools to help build and communicate mathematical understanding. *Journal of Computers in Mathematics and Science Teaching, 18*(2), 145-156.

Wittrock, M. C. (2010). Learning as a generative process. *Educational Psychologist, 45*(1), 40-45. doi:10.1080/00461520903433554

—. (1974). Learning as a generative process. *Educational Psychologist, 11*(2), 87.

Wood, D., Underwood, J., & Avis, P. (1999). Integrated learning systems in the classroom. *Computers & Education, 33*(2-3), 91-108. doi:10.1016/S0360-1315(99)00027-5

Woods, J. D., & Fraser, B. J. (1995). Reflections in teaching: What critical friends need to be able to do to stay friends. *25th Annual Conference of the Australian Association for Research in Education,*

World Economic Forum. (2002). *The global information technology report 2001-2002: Readiness for the networked world.* USA: Oxford University Press Inc.

World Economic Forum, Kirkman, G., Cornelius, P. K., Sachs, J. D., & Schwab, K. (2001). *The global information technology report 2001-2002: Readiness for the networked world (world economic forum).* USA: Oxford University Press Inc.

Zazelenchuk, T. W. (1997). Interactivity in multimedia: Reconsidering our perspective. *Canadian Journal of Educational Communication, 26*(2), 75-86.

Zhang, D., Zhao, J. L., Zhou, L., Nunamaker, J., & Jay, F. (2004). Can e-Learning replace classroom learning? *Commun. ACM, 47*(5), 75-79.

Ziguras, C. (2001). Educational technology in transnational higher education in south east asia: The cultural politics of flexible learning. *Educational Technology & Society, 4*(4), 8.

Zito, A. R., & Schout, A. (2009). Learning theory reconsidered: EU integration theories and learning. *Journal of European Public Policy, 16*(8), 1103-1123. doi:10.1080/13501760903332597

Zuga, K. F. (2004). Improving technology education research on cognition. *International Journal of Technology and Design Education, 14*(1), 79-87. doi:10.1023/B:ITDE.0000007360.33705.94